ENGLISH ECCENTRIC INTERIORS

ENGLISH ECCENTRIC INTERIORS

Miranda Harrison
Photography by Steve Gorton

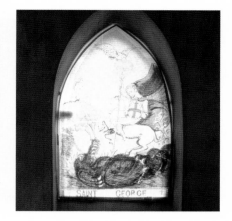

CONTENTS

ACKNOWLEDGEMENTS

So many people generously shared their time and knowledge with me during
the researching and writing of this book. Of course, buildings and interiors do
not exist in a cultural vacuum, and hundreds of intriguing facts and stories
emerged. Not all could be fitted into the pages of one volume, but to have
such a fascinating array at my disposal was an absolute pleasure and a
privilege. Dividing these acknowledgements by section, my very grateful
thanks go to:

Part I: Donna Lugg at Il Bordello; Emmanuel Tremolani at Loungelover;
Hannah Duncan at Vimac Leisure and Angela Parker and Sam Smith at the
Crab & Lobster; Michael Snodin and Anna Chalcroft at Strawberry Hill;
Simon Drake and Emma Lintern at Simon Drake's House of Magic; Kate
Kelland at the Bath House; Alan East at the Yew Tree Inn; Julian Payne and
Sue Harding at Rules.

Part II: Richard Kendall at Southside House; Sarah Philp at Charleston;
Julie Turnham at the Gothic Temple; Mick Pedroli and David Guy Milne at
Dennis Severs' House; Amy Frost (Bath Preservation Trust) and Sarah
Sampson (Landmark Trust) at Beckford's Tower & Museum; Gwen Yarker and
Shaun Garner at the Russell-Cotes Art Gallery & Museum; Mr and Mrs
Bromley-Davenport at Capesthorne Hall; Lord and Lady Digby at Minterne
House.

Part III: Medush Gupta and Marsha King at 43 South Molton Street; Peter
Henderson and Sue Geals at Three Ways House Hotel; Lou Rapley at the Old
Railway Station; Suzy Ellis and Vicky Sims at Jori White PR (for Courthouse
Hotel Kempinski); Kate Lacey (The Deco) and Steve Jones (Northampton
Jesus Centre); Richard Adams; Sally O'Loughlin and Roger Hall at the Great
John Street Hotel; Julie Arkell.

In addition, I would like to thank Minna Pang for introducing me to the
wonderful Richard Adams; Katherine Oakes at the Landmark Trust for her
considerable patience and help during the busy holiday season; and Jill
Knight, Linda Biggadike, Siôn and Joan Wynne, and Meriel and Rob Griffiths
for their generous hospitality and chauffeuring.

No acknowledgements in the *Interior Angles* series would be complete
without a huge thank you to those at and associated with Wiley-Academy,
especially Helen Castle for her vision and enthusiasm; Liz Sephton for her
elegant design; and the editorial and production prowess of Caroline Ellerby,
Abigail Grater, Mariangela Palazzi-Williams and Louise Porter.

Key to the creation of this book was, of course, the photography, and so
very grateful thanks to Steve Gorton for not only taking an inspirational set
of images, but also for driving many hundreds of miles and for such total
commitment to the project.

My final thanks go to Howard Watson. For his unwavering support and
belief in me, I dedicate this book to him.

Photo credits

Specially commissioned photography by Steve Gorton. Additional images
courtesy of: Bath Preservation Trust: 11 (bottom), 118 (top, right); Friends of
Strawberry Hill: 43 (top, right); Great John Street Hotel: 203; Jori White PR:
182 (top), 185 (top left, top right); private collection: 8 (bottom), 9 (bottom),
11 (top, right), 21 (bottom); Rules Restaurant: 70 (bottom, right), 73 (top, left).

An astonishing range of interiors, from the flamboyantly outrageous to the modestly quirky, can be found across the British Isles. Privately or publicly owned, discreetly hidden behind closed doors or thriving in the public eye, these spaces are characterised by a distinctive English eccentricity. To understand Englishness as a style is to appreciate diversity. Historically a nation of many races, Britain is unified by a strong belief in preserving traditional customs alongside an equally strong tradition of embracing individuality. From tweeds to street style, village cricket to Brit pop, old-time values and contemporary experimentation coexist in a glorious melting pot of ideas. By its very nature, therefore, Englishness can lead to eccentricity. Indeed, some may say the two concepts are hard to separate. Eccentricity is more than being singular or pushing the boundaries beyond the conventional. It requires vivacity, intelligence, a sense of occasion and a deep-rooted understanding of style and taste. In short, it needs to understand intimately the very convention that it flouts. Combined with the essential traits of Englishness, it can be the catalyst for genuine innovation and ingenuity.

Quintessentially English

Anyone with a visual interest in the world around them is likely to consider the interior of his or her home with care, but there are some who go that little bit further (or even a great deal further), for whom this space of creative potential is the perfect means of declaring all they believe in and wish to say about themselves. The same, of course, applies to public buildings, whether expressing an individual's taste or an interior that has grown organically over time. Thus, this volume includes restaurants, pubs, hotels and museums alongside a number of lesser-known treasures.

Of course, the desire to create an interior that announces an individual's idiosyncrasies to the world at large is evident in many buildings across the globe – from the colourful interiors of Roman villas to the extraordinary 21st-century ostentation of the Emirates Palace in Abu Dhabi. But what makes an interior undeniably 'English'? Analysis of this is likely to be subjective, and often results in a rather contrived thesis. Social expressions of the particularities of the English character often tell us more than the stereotypes. It is much more fun to look at what we innately feel is English and to ponder why.

Some things are obvious. For example, cuisine is an easy category with which to identify a nation. Rules, proud of its status as the oldest restaurant in London, is even more proud of its traditional English menu. Dishes of traditional game feature partridge, pheasant, wild duck, snipe, teal and roe deer from the woods and valleys of the restaurant's own country estate in the Pennines, while dessert might be bread-and-butter pudding or treacle tart and custard. The Pudding Club, housed by the Three Ways House Hotel in Gloucestershire, would no doubt thoroughly approve. Exalting such classics as jam roly-poly pudding to a status beyond any English schoolchild's wildest dreams, accommodation is offered to members and non-members alike in a typical English (Cotswold) village, in an attractive Victorian hotel with themed 'pudding rooms'.

But there are also countless restaurants, hotels and pubs across Britain that serve dishes from around the world. Indeed, the menu is often entirely international in its make-up. So with these venues, perhaps it is the interior itself that constitutes Englishness. The Crab & Lobster pub and restaurant, near Thirsk, North Yorkshire, draws on two local traditions – North Sea fishing and horseracing – as the starting points for its magical decor of assembled objects. Vast fishing nets, draped across the ceilings, are filled with all manner of things including lobster pots, shells and equestrian race cards that dangle

above The door to the Chocolate Suite at the Three Ways House Hotel is easy to spot.

below Silk restaurant at Courthouse Hotel Kempinski makes stylish use of the old courtroom.

INTRODUCTION

left A former meatpacking warehouse glistens and gleams in its new guise as Loungelover.

below Horace Walpole set priceless Flemish Early Renaissance glass into the windows of his Gothic 'castle' at Strawberry Hill.

bottom View of Strawberry Hill in 1882, which clearly shows the very different styles of Walpole's building (on the right) and Lady Waldegrave's (on the left).

above your head. Silk restaurant at Courthouse Hotel Kempinski in London features a pan-European/Asian menu but is located in an old courtroom, redolent with all the pomp and ceremony of the British legal system.

Historical Heritage

Traditions and history are key to a nation's essential characteristics. More specifically, in this book the history of English architecture and design is everywhere. An Englishman's home is always his castle – whether a worker's cottage or a stately mansion – though for centuries the English ideal has been the country house. Those who had the means, built them. And often those who did not, built them too, bankrupting themselves in the process. The splendid Stowe House in Buckinghamshire, within whose grounds the Gothic Temple resides, is a good example. By the time its proprietor was awarded a dukedom, the family had also become known as 'the greatest debtors of the world'. Exile and auctions swiftly ensued.

The sad demise of many a stately pile throughout the 20th century has been well documented, but there are still wonderful examples of country houses that have survived into the new millennium. Though some of these are still living and breathing as family homes, many have been converted for commercial use or are simply museums to a lost world.

Today the ideal of the country house manifests itself in many

ways. Luxury hotel retreats and holiday lets in obscure corners of country estates allow you to live the dream for a few days, but references to the country house and all its associated 'Englishness' can also be found in the most contemporary of spaces. 43 South Molton Street, which opened as a media-savvy central London private members' club in 2005, incorporates images of the country house (albeit painted in a bright orange) alongside framed tapestries of hunting scenes, glass cases of stuffed birds and antlers on the walls. Loungelover, also in London, does a similar thing covered in sequins.

Look at an English interior dating from before the end of the 19th century and the chances are that an earlier historical era was taken as its starting point. In Georgian London, a Roman-style Robert Adam interior became the must-have for the upper classes at a time when the discovery of Pompeii and Herculaneum had led to a flourish of Roman-inspired design and aspirations. In Warwickshire, the Bath House reflects this Classical ideal, which drew on the glories of the Roman Empire to help establish a new optimism after a century that saw plague, fire and civil war destroy much of the land and its buildings. This juxtaposition of an idealised historical style with the styles and fashions of the day creates a unique visual mix. Sometimes this mix is identified as eccentric at the time (particularly if accompanied by the flamboyant personality of its creator). Other buildings are only seen as eccentric by later viewers, when the political or social meaning might no longer be appreciated, but the resulting visual feast remains engagingly thought-provoking.

Led by pioneers such as Strawberry Hill in Middlesex, England's once all-pervading Classicism gave way to a new type of secular Gothic, which in turn led to the emergence of ever more heady fusions of styles. Beckford's Tower in Bath, for example, daringly combined Greek Revival with neo-Medievalism, while Sir John Soane, often described as England's most eccentrically brilliant architect, imbued his own brand of Neoclassicism with medieval and Baroque influences. Soane was fascinated by temples and mausoleums, and all these elements can still be seen today at his house in London's Lincoln's Inn Fields, which he designed to be his ultimate architectural legacy.

Sir John Soane died the same year that Victoria ascended the throne. Perhaps spurred on by the growing amalgamation and consolidation of the British Empire, the Victorians took the idea of fantasy history to another level. During this period interiors might be neo-Gothic, neo-Roman, Neoclassical or neo-Tudor. Influences from far-off lands were incorporated or, indeed, exploited, such as the fashionably led heavy demand for chinoiserie. Eccentric interiors might combine some or all of these influences, as in the Scottish-Baronial-meets-Moorish-palace effect at the Russell-Cotes Art Gallery & Museum mansion on the cliffs at Bournemouth.

This prolific use of styles, plus the increasingly statuesque and monumental (and therefore costly) buildings made possible by new methods and materials, dominated the English landscape until the socialist utopia of the Arts and Crafts movement reacted against it. Born out of a concern for the effects of industrialisation on traditional skills and the lives of ordinary people, it advocated design reform at every level and turned the home into a work of art. Half a century after William Morris first espoused his ideals, Vanessa Bell, at the suggestion of her sister Virginia Woolf, moved into an old cottage in Sussex. Perhaps the best-known example of turning your home into a work of art, Charleston was to be decorated and redecorated by Vanessa Bell and Duncan Grant over the next 50 years. Charming, personal and completely unique, this was a glorious 20th-century response to the call to replace the ideal of the aristocratic interior with something more accessible.

Intriguing Interiors

Today, eccentric ideas and designs come from a huge variety of influences, backed by finances from a wide range of sources. Many of the interiors featured in this book incorporate deliberate references to the tastes and styles of bygone eras, and all are united by a rich blend of vivacity and individuality. Two of them – Strawberry Hill and Minterne House – are architecturally eccentric. Built two centuries apart, both buildings display an intellectual sense of fun, a playful bending of the rules. One joyfully (and politically) adapted the English Gothic of churches large and small across the land to a totally new kind of domestic architecture for this 'little plaything house' on the Thames. The other threw together a veritable panoply of England's architectural styles, from Tudor to Arts and Crafts.

Other interiors are unique reinventions of the spaces, resulting in something entirely different to the original intention. Preserving the past need not be dull, nor indeed

below At Simon Drake's House of Magic, his Auditorium is set within a Gothic fantasy of *trompe l'oeil* tracery and curtain swags, with roses winding up the wrought iron banisters.

above left John Landseer at Russell-Cotes Art Gallery & Museum.

above right The fearsome fire at Capesthorne Hall appeared on the front page of *The Illustrated London News* on 12th October 1861.

below Exterior view of Beckford's Tower, painted in 1844 by Willes Maddox.

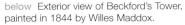

subservient to prevailing tastes. Il Bordello (now a members-only bar) was once a Dutch coal barge; Courthouse Hotel Kempinski was, as the name suggests, a magistrates' court; and beautifully restored Pullman carriages make marvellous bedrooms at the Old Railway Station bed and breakfast.

Elsewhere, interiors are simply flamboyant expressions of the life and work of the owners. Richard Adams' house is an exuberant showpiece for an interior designer, Charleston is the quintessential artists' house, and Simon Drake's House of Magic (a private residence and theatrical venue) blurs the boundaries between domestic and theatrical as only a magician could.

Then there are the very public expressions of eccentricity. Loungelover basks in its glorious individuality, Dennis Severs' House is a masterpiece of theatrical history, and the Three Ways House Hotel delights in playing genial host to the activities of the Pudding Club. The Russell-Cotes Art Gallery & Museum, although initially a home, was always intended to become a museum, and its deliberate flamboyance was nothing less than showy ostentation. The Yew Tree Inn, on the other hand, simply combines one person's love of antiques with his job as a publican.

Another type of interior in this volume is that which survives today by leading a double life in the modern world. On one floor, Beckford's Tower has a charming little museum of William Beckford's life and work run by the Bath Preservation Trust, while the old service quarters below now house a particularly adventurous Landmark Trust conversion to luxury holiday accommodation. Going a stage further, the stunning auditorium of a former Art Deco cinema now operates as The Deco conference centre, theatre and multipurpose venue when its facilities are being managed by a corporate entertainment company, and as the Northampton Jesus Centre when the local branch of the Jesus Army is using it for worship. Paring back the complexities of modern use to get back to each of the buildings as a whole has been a privilege.

Finally, a number of the interiors have a modesty and charm that belies their strength and individuality. Capesthorne Hall, with its mural-decorated theatre, bedrooms of family items, and themed collections, has a quiet allure beneath which it has staunchly resisted fire and misfortune, while at Julie Arkell's house, a building that has been lived in by her family since 1919, the apparent clutter and chaos is, in fact, a steadfast and unwavering expression of the artist's work and her beliefs.

Whatever the reason for considering these interiors as essentially English, the one thing they most certainly are not is reserved. Eccentricity in all its many guises is given free rein to romp and carouse through the limitless powers of the imagination.

ECCENTRIC ENTERTAINMENT

Where better to throw a party or celebrate good news than in an interior that is imbued with a sense of fun, and rejoices in being unorthodox? Bringing together a selection of interiors that share an obvious enjoyment of the world they inhabit, this section celebrates a pleasure-seeking and vivacious strand of eccentricity.

Entertainment and eccentricity are a natural coupling and, of course, both have long been a part of English life. The playful interior of the Bath House in Warwickshire, its ceiling festooned with plaster icicles and its walls decorated by swags of shellwork, was designed for the amusement of guests as they stopped for picnics or tea parties during the long walk through the extensive estate of Walton Hall. Twenty years later, Horace Walpole had completed the Long Gallery at Strawberry Hill in Twickenham and was hosting lavish entertainments in his 'castle'. In a letter to his friend George Montague, he wrote excitedly in 1769: 'Strawberry has been in great glory – I have given a festino there that will almost mortgage it … I greeted [the guests] dressed in the cravat of Gibbons' carving and a pair of French gloves embroidered up to the elbows that had belonged to James I.' Evidently he saw himself, as well as his glorious fan-vaulted gallery, as part of the entertainment.

Some of the interiors in this section display a distinctly salacious appetite for entertainment. Not surprisingly, given its name, Il Bordello in Bristol is one such space. It luxuriates in sensuous colours and textures, surrounding the cocktail drinker with a glorious fusion of black, red and pink. Scantily clad women and smoking sailor boys are painted on the lavatory doors, adding a humorous touch

ECCENTRIC

of suggestiveness. The decadence of East London's Loungelover lies more in the tactile mix of objects and furniture. It is a place that loves to love, with its name emblazoned in sparkling jewels upon the wall and cinematic lighting casting a rich glow upon proceedings. Simon Drake's House of Magic is another space that stimulates the senses, with its Whispering Chair, Haunted Cellar and Red Room. Exuding a tongue-in-cheek Gothic horror, both this London house and its owner provide a flamboyant, cheeky style of entertainment. Meanwhile, something distinctly saucy is taking place in the gentlemen's lavatories at the Crab & Lobster in North Yorkshire. Away from the glorious clutter of old-style bric-a-brac, vintage clothing, books, lobster pots, musical instruments, puppets on strings and so on that dominate the bar and the dining areas, the lavatories provide a haven of calm contemplation of the female form.

Another venue in this section to feature an amazing clutter of objects is the Yew Tree Inn in Staffordshire. Here the collection is united by the tastes of the antique-loving publican, and includes some extremely collectable and valuable items. The pub itself is 17th-century, and provides a dimly lit and low-ceilinged backdrop to the dark woods of antique furniture and clocks. Many of the objects are to do with musical entertainment, including a gramophone, a pianola and several very tall Victorian musical instruments (symphonions and polyphons) that, much to the delight of the punters, are in full working order. All the antiques are mixed in together with the modern paraphernalia of pub life, creating an engaging miscellany within which to sit and have a drink.

At the end of the 20th century, Rules, the final venue in this section, celebrated 200 years of wining and dining actors, writers, artists, lawyers, journalists and other such professionals in the heart of London's West End. The restaurant's location made it an obvious haunt of entertainers and the entertained – from Henry Irving to Laurence Olivier, Charles Dickens to Graham Greene, and Charlie Chaplin to John Barrymore. Hundreds of drawings, paintings, cartoons, letters and playbills are framed in a wonderful hotchpotch upon the walls, making this unofficial 'green room' of the world of entertainment a truly remarkable space. With its themed dining rooms based on four of its most well-known and loyal diners, and its traditional English menu of game, oysters, pies and puddings, Rules provides a fascinating link to the past, yet thrives in the contemporary desire for the stylishly unorthodox.

above Copper pans, hats, parasols, toys and all manner of antique objects hang above the dining tables at the Crab & Lobster, while dressers, cupboards and bookcases jostle for wall space with prints and ceramics.

ENTERTAINMENT

name
    Il Bordello
address
    Welshback, Bristol BS1 4RS
telephone
    0117 925 3500
website
    www.ilbordello.co.uk
opening times
    Tuesday: 6pm–1am (also open to non-members); Wednesday to Saturday: 6pm–2am (open to non-members for certain events). Open from midday in summer months
description
    Members' bar on a barge
original structure
    Dutch barge, 1925
interior
    Liz Lewitt, 2002
design style
    1930s nautical meets kitsch bordello

Stroll past Il Bordello in the summer months, and this former coal-carrying Dutch barge looks nothing more than an attractive floating bar, with chairs and tables dotted about the upper deck and a bright awning adding colour and shade. But step inside, and you descend a golden staircase into the cheekily decadent world that is Il Bordello.

Highly appropriately, Il Bordello is located in a city that, by the 13th century, had decided that wine should be its main import. Bristol's port boomed in the late 17th century, as its location on the west coast was ideal for trade with the new colonies founded in the West Indies and North America. A less appealing side of this was the slave trade, from which the city profited heavily in the 18th century. Shipbuilding, brewing and the chocolate industry were major concerns at this time. The Industrial Revolution resulted in Bristol being connected to London by rail in 1841, and the pioneering construction of the suspension bridge at Clifton in 1864.

Drawing inspiration from sources such as rustic Italy and the 1930s, with a mix of North African materials and New York graffiti thrown in for good measure, the glorious interior of Il Bordello is a mix of intimate and funky. Appropriately, given the venue's name, the decorative scheme is a blend of hedonistic red and black.

Built in 1925, the barge was a hard-working commercial craft in Holland before it was brought to the UK. Many Bristolians remember its subsequent use

above A key element of Il Bordello's branding is the red rose.

opposite Designed by owner Liz Lewitt (her background in fashion design included lingerie collections for Agent Provocateur), Il Bordello is a popular members' club for Bristol's media cognoscenti.

IL BORDELLO

17

as the spit-and-sawdust home of a motorbike club – with no lavatories. At nearly 30 metres (98 feet) long, however, there was scope for adding a kitchen at one end and unisex loos at the other.

Much of the craft's riveted-steel interior can still be seen, albeit coated in a deep shade of red. The curved planked ceiling and tongue-and-groove walls share the same deep red, which is pierced on one side by light streaming in through small portholes. A mass of fairy lights was once hung across a section of the ceiling for a party, and has remained there ever since. The effect is reminiscent of glinting silver fish caught in a net. The furniture suggests an old-style gentlemen's club – dark wooden chairs upholstered in black leather, and squashy black leather sofas. At Il Bordello, however, you'll find the sofas adorned with cushions of assorted shades of pink and red, in fabrics ranging from faux fur to Indian silk.

The theme of black leather set against splashes of colour is picked up again at the bar, where leather panels provide a dark contrast to the dangling coloured light bulbs above. This is a bar for cocktails and champagne – beer drinkers have to be content with bottled beer, as a flat-bottomed boat has no cellars! Recesses and ledges created by the barge's steel structure make unusual shelving for wine glasses and bottles of cocktail ingredients, while the ubiquitous chrome cocktail accessories sit well with a large 1930s-style fan that dominates the bar counter.

opposite, above Artworks by Nick Walker are reflected in the lavatory mirrors.

opposite, below The interior is constantly changed by featuring regular art exhibitions on its walls. This work, by Jud, sits snugly between the portholes.

bottom The moulded steel of the original coal barge has been cleverly utilised to store bottles and glasses at the bar.

below Coloured light bulbs add an unexpected glow of colour above the bar.

Tucked away in the corner opposite the bar is a strangely decorated ledge, with tall black stools underneath. The design, comprising a collage of roses, is hardly noticeable in the dark corner, but would be a fun discovery after a few drinks at the bar. And indeed, after a few at the bar you will probably start to wonder where the lavatories are. Up at the entrance end of the boat, they lurk behind a sliding silver door where the original galley kitchen would have been located. These are lavatories not to be missed. Two cubicle doors are adorned with paintings of scantily clad women, while two more depict smoking sailor boys. Painted by celebrated graffiti artist Nick Walker, they provide a wonderful touch of humour and suggestiveness.

Nick Walker's art has also featured in the regularly changing programme of exhibitions on the walls of Il Bordello, which in recent months have ranged from huge posters to small, black-framed works by Jud. Billed on its website as an 'arts and performance bar and late lounge', this is a venue that encourages proposals for exhibitions, hosting openings as well as independently curated evenings.

Returning once more to the staircase, the ascent is made glorious by the use of golden tiles set into the steps. More champagne than brassy, this gold appears

opposite Inlaid with gold tiles, the staircase provides a flamboyant exit to the top deck.

above The nautical and the naughty are all part of the fun at Il Bordello.

below 'Burlesque goes Bawdy' flyer.

elsewhere on the barge as delicate touches such as thread in a cushion cover or a motif on a stool. At the top of the stairs the door is painted with a *trompe l'oeil* effect (Nick Walker again) to make it look as if it is padded in black leather. Linking back to the decor below, this fun evocation of luxury brings to mind opulent interiors from the 1930s (interestingly, having a padded leather door was a sign of status during the communist era). Communist officials would, no doubt, have thoroughly appreciated the chance to unwind in the sensuous decadence of Il Bordello's themed night, 'Burlesque goes Bawdy'.

For those with specific musical tastes, the 'Gimme Shelter' night features 1960s rhythm and blues, soul, beat, Tamla, jazz and go-go, while the weekly 'Latin Lounge' has DJs, live musicians and a lively crowd taking full advantage of the two-for-one Havana Rum cocktails. If none of these whet your appetite, there is always the 'Sad Café', promoting soft-rock anthems and power ballads as 'the music you hate to love'. It's all in the name of fun, and this splendidly eccentric venue is just the place to let your hair down.

name
  Loungelover

address
  2 Whitby Street, London E1 6JU

telephone
  020 7010 1234

website
  www.loungelover.co.uk

opening times
  Tuesday to Saturday: 6pm–midnight

description
  Cocktail lounge

original structure
  19th-century warehouse

interior
  Hassan Abdullah, 2003

design style
  Rustic European meets antique and
  modern kitsch

above Greeting you at the door is this cheeky card-bearing frog, with jaunty butterfly wired to his body.

When restaurant Les Trois Garçons opened in London in 2000, its joyful celebration of maximalism caused quite a furore, as did the living arrangements of the three boys in question. Three years later, the same triumvirate opened Loungelover, an eccentrically extravagant cocktail bar located in a former meatpacking warehouse. You would be unlikely to find the luxurious dimensions of such a warehouse in Bond Street or Mayfair. Loungelover borders on the now achingly hip district of Shoreditch. This is not the East End of dodgy pubs and the criminal underworld of the Kray twins. The 'cafe society' has moved in, creating an East End that is a fun and funky place to eat, drink, visit an art gallery or buy a converted modern apartment to make your home. Recent restoration of some houses in Hackney has revealed buildings that look as if they could be in Georgian Islington or Victorian Hampstead.

opposite Rustic furniture in the foreground gives way to an eccentric mix of styles – a pink 1960s sofa amidst Baroque-style chairs is placed in front of anatomical posters.

On entering Loungelover, the first impression is one of dazzling light and colour. Adjust your eyes to the immediate foreground and a smiling frog comes into view. Behind him, a long, French refectory table is surrounded by assorted rustic Swedish chairs. On the table stands a series of exceptionally tall wineglass vases, each containing a green wreath with tiny pink flowers. This area is clearly designed for a group, but just feet away the layout is more private. Here, in the flamboyant Baroque Lounge area, curvaceous chairs gather round a blancmange-pink 1960s sofa. Glorying in its plasticity, it stands below posters of anatomical drawings – anyone who has seen Gunther von Hagens' 'Bodyworlds' exhibition will find these hard to disassociate from his plastination process. Fleetingly, a more gruesome interpretation of 'meatpacking' comes to mind, but it is hard to be serious in the presence of sparkling lettering and dangling merry-go-round horses.

below The old ceiling and walls of the meatpacking warehouse provide a textured backdrop for sparkling stags' heads, old eastern European carousel horses, and a bejewelled 'Lover' sign.

LOUNGELOVER

23

Nearby, a 1960s tubular Murano-glass concoction is the first of several large and highly individual chandeliers that herald each new space in the lounge bar. To the right of the pink sofa, full-length curtains signify a change of pace. Lavender-upholstered medallion furniture is positioned beneath a glorious old chandelier that once hung in a Cannes casino. A vast, cracked oil-painted cartoon for an Aubusson tapestry adds an intriguing architectural dimension to the setting, while elaborate bronze candleholders continue the theme of Baroque excess.

Opposite the historical drama of the tapestry cartoon is a gloriously bizarre tableau. An old wooden doll's house, stripped of its internal walls and filled with tea lights, sits on a huge 19th-century French buffet. This splendidly carved piece of furniture runs the length of a wall that separates the lounge from the kitchen. Green glass and metal aquatic creatures conjure up a fish-tank effect, while earthenware pots containing large leaves extend the fish-tank illusion around the doll's house. This creates a fun and quirky space in an area where the atmosphere might have fallen flat. The kitchen, offering a brasserie-style menu, is boxed in, with huge Victorian lanterns fixed above the green-glass panel and stuffed deer standing on its ceiling. No part of Loungelover has been overlooked in its rich and playful decor.

Affectionately known as 'the cage', the Private Room is the only space in the lounge bar that is enclosed by three walls. Folded within the pillars on either side of the alcove are wrought-iron gates, the former shopfront of a French butcher's. These can be unfolded and shut if privacy is required; the space is available

above Dazzling light fittings are a key feature of Loungelover. Here, the glass fronds of an old Cannes casino chandelier hang above a battered cartoon for an Aubusson tapestry.

below A doll's house filled with tea lights draws the eye to the green glass of the faux fish tank that divides the lounge bar from the kitchen.

right French rustic furniture includes a cabinet filled with cobweb-festooned Courvoisier and Ballantynes bottles.

exclusively to members. Here, fairy lights glisten on side tables, while ranged around a huge wooden swan and a Friesian cowhide pouffe is Swedish and French furniture from the 18th and 19th centuries. On the back wall, an explosion of colourful stained glass and jewels fills a stunning piece of carved oak that looks as if it once held a mirror. Two rustic French cabinets display, on the one side, Courvoisier and Ballantynes bottles alongside chunky ceramics, and on the other side a glorious set of Lulu Guinness handbags at their most whimsical, with designs ranging from fairytale castle to bucket of roses.

Back in the main lounge bar, more rustic French cabinets are stacked with wines, conveniently located beside the actual bar. The motif of using the single word 'Lover', seen in the Baroque Lounge area, is repeated here in large bronze lettering above the counter, while silk flowers and a Victorian pub lantern

above A mannequin observes the action from his ship-lit corner.

right The Private Room is a veritable curiosity shop of artefacts.

complete the picture. Tall glass vases sit alongside bulbous bronze planters, and the nature theme is carried through to the gnarled-branch effect of the stools ranged in front of the bar. Reflected in the polished counter is a strong red hue, coming from the final section of the lounge bar, known as the Red Lounge.

Draped with red dress-lining fabric, the walls of this area become a vibrant canvas on which to play with colour and light. Chandeliers made from coronets hang suspended in front of the vivid chequered window, elaborate sidelights sparkle at the central chandelier, and studio spotlights add to the theatre of the space. With retro club furnishings, including red plastic stools, glass-topped tables and even a hostess trolley, this is the ultimate cocktail-drinking environment. You may be tempted by Ten Times A Lady (Plymouth fruit cup, passion fruit and Miller's gin topped with Prosecco), or perhaps Original Sin (green apple, honey and horseradish-flavoured Sputnik Russian vodka, shaken with a dash of lemon) would be more appropriate.

Fantastically flamboyant and outrageously eccentric, Loungelover has become a firm favourite with London's celebrity, fashion and media culture, as well as a discerning local clientele. This is a space in which to marvel as you party.

above left The bar is surrounded by a mix of pots and glass, artworks and old salvaged iron.

above The theatricality of the Red Lounge is manifest in the red drapes, the chandelier that was rescued from a condemned Art Deco theatre near Brighton, and the studio spotlights.

name
Crab & Lobster/Crab Manor Hotel

address
Dishforth Road, Asenby, Thirsk, North
Yorkshire Y07 3QL

telephone
01845 577286

website
www.crabandlobster.com

opening times
Pub: 11am–11pm

description
Pub and restaurant, and luxury hotel

original structure
Pub: 17th-century thatched cottage.
Hotel: Georgian house

interior
Pub: Jackie and David Barnard, 1990.
Hotel: various, 1999 onwards

design style
Eclectic mix of nautical and historical
ephemera

Just south of Asenby in the heart of 'Herriot Country', gateway to the Yorkshire Dales and North York Moors, is a crossroads where two small signs, each bearing a crab and a lobster, point in completely opposite directions. On closer inspection, it becomes apparent that one directs you to the Crab & Lobster, while the other indicates Crab Manor. On foot they are actually very close to each other, separated only by a short walk through landscaped gardens. Housed in a 17th-century thatched building, the Crab & Lobster has enjoyed many years' success as a distinctly unusual pub and restaurant. Just as decoratively adventurous is

CRAB & LOBSTER / CRAB MANOR HOTEL

opposite A window seat in the pub section of the Crab & Lobster, resembling a cosy, cluttered Victorian parlour.

below View across the bar, with its books stuffed below the counter and horse-racing tickets hanging from the ceiling.

the Crab Manor Hotel, a Georgian house set in three adjoining hectares (seven acres). Both venues are now run by northeast-based leisure-management company Vimac Leisure, which loved the interiors so much that it based its refurbishments on the original themes.

Befitting its thatched-cottage exterior, the Crab & Lobster combines an attractive medley of domestic ephemera with antique objects. In the window of the pub section, suitcases, champagne bottles, tins, old cameras and a sewing machine sit alongside a stuffed cockatoo in a glass-fronted case. The green-and-white tablecloths have a country-cottage feel to them, while draped up above are large swathes of fishing net, filled with a jumble of beer mats, bottles, shells, magazines and equestrian race cards. Many and various old books are stuffed in a recess in the bar counter, beside which an old map of North Yorkshire is propped up behind a Tiffany-style lamp. A bust of Napoleon guards the beer pumps, and a wooden crocodile watches proceedings from a prime position at the bar. Over on a wobbly Rococo-style table, generously sized champagne bottles are sandwiched between two old accordions, beneath a lavishly framed still life.

This genteel eccentricity does little to prepare you for the extraordinary gentlemen's lavatories – a veritable shrine to Marilyn Monroe. From all over the walls she beams at you, and in the single cubicle she is positively raunchy. A wooden rack (of the type found in old kitchens, lowered by a rope in order to access pots and pans) hangs from the ceiling, from which assorted items of ladies' lingerie dangle decorously. On the other side of the room, a Classical cast of writhing figures provides an odd contrast to the Hollywood glamour of Ms Monroe.

One wonders which icon of the 20th century is to be worshipped in the women's lavatories, but, instead, an entirely different ambience greets the female customer. More like the changing room in a vintage clothes shop than a lavatory, the room is dominated by a mannequin standing beside the basin, complete with extraordinarily large hat and fur stole worn over a long silk dress. An old Harrods clothes box leans against the wall. Against the willow-pattern wallpaper, swathes of fabric draped over the mirror and central light create an effect that is almost that of a state bedroom, but the dense collage of articles and cuttings from women's magazines on the ceiling makes sure that any aristocratic flights of fancy are swiftly brought back into a world of coupons and sewing patterns.

This suggestion of times past appears to have been taken up in the restaurant with rampant abandon, but the effect is one of endless intrigue rather than a claustrophobic onslaught. The theme of fishing nets draped across the ceiling and filled with assorted items is taken up here with more exuberance. Where in the pub you might spy beer mats and bottles in the nets, here you are more likely to observe

top The walls of the men's lavatories are covered with pictures of Marilyn Monroe.

above Vintage clothing, fabric drapes, a willow-pattern wallpaper and a ceiling papered with images from women's magazines greet the female lavatory visitor.

above The restaurant is crammed full of antiques, many suspended from netting that covers the ceiling.

below right Ice skates, a puppet and even a cello have found their way into the restaurant's amazing ceiling collage.

below left Battered screens and shelves of ephemera create individual spaces within the restaurant.

copper pots and vintage hats. Vying with the nets are touches such as a teddy bear of the fluffiest kind sitting innocently in the toothy jaw of a stag's head. Meanwhile, dressers, cupboards and bookcases jostle for wall space with items such as nautical prints, equestrian saddles and plates. Amidst all this, elegantly dressed tables invite the diner to join in the fun. A window offers natural light into an area that has a slightly more open-plan approach to seating, but most of the restaurant dining is based in cosy enclosures created by battered screens or heavy furniture.

One side of the restaurant leads into the Pavilion, a brighter room that introduces new colour and light to the space. Red, orange, yellow and cream strips of canvas and bunting create a tent-like effect across the ceiling, culminating in a central cross of wooden beams. Nautical items such as a rubber ring and model boats swing from the crossbeam, and swooping down into the action an antique diving suit surveys the scene below. As in the previous two rooms, the window sills are filled with old books, tins, lamp bases and so on, and candles adorn every table.

Upstairs is a room that can be used for smaller, more private gatherings. Rich burgundy walls add a warm cosiness to this room. The style is still one of a vintage quirkiness, but the space is calmer. A sense of nostalgia is introduced by assorted hats hanging out of wooden drawers, hat boxes and books piled up,

above The Pavilion, a modern extension of the restaurant, continues the theme of antiques and knick-knacks on every surface, but opens up the space with big picture windows and brightly coloured canvas across the ceiling.

opposite Above the restaurant, a more private space can be hired. The nautical theme continues with lobster pots in the netting.

above right Looking for that elusive lobster.

and a seamstress's dummy propped up in the corner. This ceiling's netting includes sheet music and a lobster pot.

Behind the Crab & Lobster, a path and steps lead up to the gravel drive of Crab Manor. Here, the emphasis is on luxury, with each room designed to transport you into the decor of some of the world's most famous hotels. With room names including the Waldorf Astoria, Raffles, the Cipriani, Turnberry, Sharrow Bay and Sandy Lane, this is a worldwide cruise indeed.

The front door opens into an elegant hall with rounded Georgian arches. Sturdy dark furniture displays an assortment of silverware and ceramics; white painted stucco contrasts with the burgundy and gold wallpaper. But the initial impression of sanity is deceptive. An 8-kilogramme (18-pound) pike in a glass case shares the same wall as a hall stand sporting teddy bears, and an utterly

top The yeti at the top of the stairs.

above Bird Island Lodge has a permanent resident.

above right In the hotel, the initial impression of serenity is deceiving – bizarre objects adorn the walls.

bizarre – and very large – creature stands at the top of the first flight of stairs. It is a model yeti, which once resided in the York Dungeon. The staff still laugh about the extraordinary sight of the huge beast being driven to Crab Manor on the roof of the owner's car. Perhaps a rather more attractive feature of the landing is the very large, rusty clock. Made in Havana, US, in the 1930s, it might be more at home with the diving suit than the yeti – but it is precisely this sort of unexpected coupling that makes this place so intriguing.

Doors all around the yeti lead to the themed bedrooms, but there are also rooms in the grounds of Crab Manor. Curiously, two suites are set into an authentic tropical beach house, creating a fantasy retreat from the North Yorkshire climate. Both suites have a decked terrace and a Californian-style hot-

above The Bird Island room is the most
exotic of the 'world cruise' bedrooms.

tub jacuzzi. The Bird Island Lodge suite is a truly sumptuous visual feast. Fun
elements include green bamboo-print wallpaper, thatched matting along narrow
shelving, and a gloriously tropical curtain, cushion and wallpaper design of
elaborate foliage and huge pink flowers. Coral-coloured sheeting is draped in
pleats across the ceiling, culminating in a light fitting with flamboyant twists of
wire that suggest the plumage of exotic birds. Artefacts imported from the
Seychelles add an authentic touch; for example, the wood and wire birdcage,
painted an ivory colour, with various fabric and wooden birds attached. And who
could fail to be excited by the large carved wooden monkey, with a garland
around its neck, who stands near the door of the sauna as if guarding the heat
from the cold outside.

name
   Strawberry Hill
address
   Strawberry Hill, Waldegrave Road,
   Twickenham TW1 4SX
telephone
   020 8240 4224
website
   www.friendsofstrawberryhill.org
opening times
   Public tours: every Sunday, May to
   September (2pm, 2.45pm and 3.30pm).
   Private tours: every day except
   Saturdays
description
   Early example of Gothic Revival
original structure
   17th-century riverside villa
interior
   Walpole building: Horace Walpole,
   John Chute, Richard Bentley and
   others, mid-18th-century
design style
   Fantasy Gothic castle

In the 18th century, Twickenham was a resort for fashionable society. Located between the palaces of Kew and Hampton Court, in a pretty countryside setting on the river Thames, it was the perfect place for summer entertainment. Famous residents included the poet Alexander Pope and the celebrated comic actress Kitty Clive. In 1747, Horace Walpole moved to a Thames-side house that was owned by the proprietress of a famous London toy shop. Built by a coachman 50 years earlier, the house had been dubbed 'Chopp'd Straw Hall'. This was pure snobbery, inferring that the coachman could only have made his money by selling off good-quality hay intended for his employer's horses and giving them inferior 'chopped' straw instead. Whatever the circumstances of its origins, the house greatly appealed to Walpole. In typically flamboyant manner, he wrote to his cousin in June 1747: 'It is a little plaything-house that I got out of Mrs Chenevix's [toy] shop and is the prettiest bauble you ever saw … Pope's ghost is just now skimming under the window by a most poetical moonlight.'

The youngest son of Sir Robert Walpole, Britain's first prime minister, Horace was a compulsive collector, a keen observer of the social mores of the day and a prolific correspondent. Caught up in the rise of Romanticism (where strong emotions such as trepidation, awe and horror could be seen as aesthetic experiences), he also relished the new appreciation of medieval Gothic church architecture, tomb sculpture, stained glass and so on. This twin interest became known as 'Gothick', an aesthetic that was intimately bound up with the pursuit of something mysterious, unearthly, and not a little theatrical. It began to appear in design, manifesting itself in buildings such as the 'Gothick' temple at Stowe (see separate section).

Having purchased the Twickenham house and christened it Strawberry Hill, after the local name for its 2-hectare (5-acre) estate, Walpole set about creating

opposite The Library door opens into a passageway with characteristic Gothic window and stained glass.

below The entrance hall's staircase, designed by Richard Bentley, is based on the library staircase at Rouen Cathedral. The arches of its Gothic tracery are echoed by the pointed arches of the doorways.

STRAWBERRY HILL

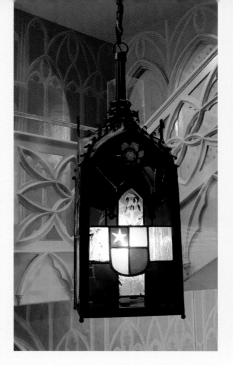

his vision of a fantasy Gothic castle. On completion it was double the house's original size, with battlements, pinnacles, quatrefoil windows, fan vaulting and towers. Not only did it deliberately lack the order and symmetry of the prevailing Classicism, but its Gothic style was far from a pure rendition of its medieval antecedent. His creation was to become one of the most influential houses in the history of English architecture.

Since Walpole's death its history has been chequered, but thankfully it is still standing (albeit somewhat shakily), and funding has just been awarded for a major programme of restoration.

Today, the entrance hall is a splendid example of how Walpole's original has been affected by subsequent alterations. The pink tracery wallpaper dates from the 1950s. While it reflects the Gothic tracery seen all over the house, the colour is a far cry from Walpole's desired 'gloomth' (his own word). He wrote with obvious satisfaction in a letter of June 1753 that he had filled the lantern 'with painted glass, which casts the most venerable gloom on the stairs that was seen since the days of Abelard'. Picture the same staircase and balustrade against a dark-grey paper taking its design from a cathedral tomb, and the Gothic becomes more obvious.

The blue-and-gold decoration of the stairwell ceiling was a Victorian addition, in an attempt to 'de-gloom', as was the replacing of the hexagonal stone floor tiles with beautiful Minton tiles. To design historians these Victorian elements are just as interesting – but for the particular subversion of earlier styles that is a part of this book's English eccentricity, it is Walpole's Strawberry Hill that is the star.

In his inimitable style, Walpole set up a 'Committee of Taste' to create his

above left The pink entrance hall would be just as startling to Walpole as it is to us. His intention was to create a dark, tomb-like interior.

above middle View of a corner of the Library.

above right The ceiling was designed by Walpole to commemorate his ancestry in the Crusades. This is Fitz Osbert on horseback.

opposite, above The Saracen's head motif appears all over the house in various forms. Here it sits above the fireplace in the Parlour, with a 1950s strawberry wallpaper behind that was based on a design by the great Gothic revivalist AWN Pugin.

opposite, below The Library is a spectacularly original example of the new 'Gothick' styling.

Gothic fantasy. Its original members were Walpole himself, naturally, John Chute (who designed a bold mix of Classical and Gothic interiors at his family seat, the Vyne in Hampshire) and Richard Bentley, illustrator and writer (nicknamed 'the Goth' by Walpole). These amateur enthusiasts were joined by William Robinson, from the board of works, to oversee structural and building matters.

Despite altered colour schemes and the insertion of cupboards where once bookshelves were floor length, the Library is still a breathtaking spectacle. Chute drew on a Wenceslaus Hollar engraving of Old St Paul's for the pierced Gothic arches of the bookcases, and the chimney piece was based on a tomb in Westminster Abbey.

The ceiling was designed by Walpole. The Saracen's head crest of the Walpole family was supposedly granted in 1191 to a Walpole who fought at the

Siege of Acre during the Crusades. Walpole used it liberally around the house, including on this ceiling. He loved stories of his ancestors in the Crusades, and two of them are commemorated here.

Walpole is known to many fans of the genre as the author of the first Gothic novel. His transformation of Strawberry Hill provided the inspiration for *The Castle of Otranto*, which he wrote in 1764 after a particularly vivid dream. It set the style for every Gothic tale thereafter, where terror is inseparable from the architecture of halls, stairways, chambers, closets, secret passages and dungeons.

This author of Gothic horror, however, was the same man who delighted in lavish entertainments in his opulent Long Gallery. Completed the year before the novel, the gallery was a brand new addition to the original house, stretching away from Walpole's more personal quarters and designed as an elaborate showpiece for the

above The spectacular fan vaulting of the Long Gallery ceiling is made of papier-mâché.

opposite, left View into the mirror above the fireplace in the Long Gallery.

opposite, right The Long Gallery was a dazzling place to entertain, with candles reflecting in the angled mirrors. There were no shutters on the windows opposite, allowing sunlight and moonlight to pour into the room.

above left Through the Gothic arches of the window and the tracery design below can be seen the Victorian facade of Lady Waldegrave's wing.

above right The purple and white of the Holbein Room is the original colour scheme.

opposite The green and gold fan vaulting of the Tribune, a room designed to display the most prized objects in Walpole's collection.

below Throughout the house, Walpole's stained glass was embellished with floral designs in the 1950s.

best items of his extensive collection. Chute's exquisite fan vaulting immediately recalls that of its acknowledged source, Henry VII's chapel at Westminster Abbey. Like much of Strawberry Hill at this time, this was decoration rather than structure. Made entirely of papier-mâché, it had miraculously survived for nearly 200 years when it narrowly escaped destruction during extensive war-time bombing.

The canopies above the recesses were designed by a new member of the Committee of Taste, Thomas Pitt. Bentley had been eased out by this time, partly due to Walpole's dislike of his wife. The combination of Gothic fan vaulting, gold Islamic-inspired fretwork, mirrors and red silk damask creates an extraordinary room that continues to dazzle its visitors. At one end is the Tribune.

Named by Walpole after the room in Florence's Uffizi Palace where all the best treasures were kept, the Tribune was the highlight of any discerning visitor's tour of his house. Here he kept priceless miniatures and enamels, coins and medals. The ceiling was loosely inspired by the Chapterhouse at York Minster. In the 1920s, when the house became a priests' seminary, this room was consecrated and used as a private chapel right up to their departure in 1992.

By 1856, when the house had passed to Lady Frances Waldegrave, Strawberry Hill had become quite derelict (parts of the building are still only timber-framed with a skin of render). Boosted by funds from her third marriage, Lady Waldegrave decided to restore and expand it. She introduced a number of practical alterations to the layout of the house (the antithesis of Walpole's whimsical lack of order), brightened the entrance hall as described earlier, and installed an opulent floor from a Viennese villa in the Long Gallery. She then built a new wing, containing a ballroom and dining room, at right angles to the Long Gallery. Its facade can be seen through Walpole's Gothic gallery windows.

Back in the original house, Walpole's stunning purple-and-white Holbein Room, so named because of its collection of Holbeins and tracings of Holbein drawings, is another glorious exposition in Gothick. Bentley based the screen partition on one at Rouen Cathedral that was subsequently destroyed, supporting Walpole's declaration that his use of Gothic objects as inspiration could sometimes be 'the sole preservative' of their style. Once again, the ceiling is papier-mâché, and the splendid chimney piece was based on a tomb at Canterbury Cathedral.

Other rooms in the original house that now sport a mixture of styles include the Parlour, the Refectory, the Tower Room and the various bed chambers. The one room that Lady Waldegrave changed completely was the Breakfast Room. Subsequently known as the Turkish Boudoir, this is a wonderful example of Lady Waldegrave's desire to add her own personality to the house. Husbands three and four were great friends of Edward Lear, who travelled and painted in Turkey, and it is thought that his watercolours may have inspired the Turkish motifs. Spectacular ceiling embroideries and thick curtains contribute to the atmosphere of a secret tryst.

In Walpole's day, this room was papered in blue-and-white stripes, and was a particular favourite for its views of the Thames. The windows are Walpole's originals, dating from his earliest work on the house. The stained glass is the oldest in the house, and its rich blue setting would have been a carefully considered part of the blue-and-white scheme.

Today, Strawberry Hill moves into an exciting new phase as tireless campaigning for urgently needed restoration is finally starting to pay off. Walpole would be both astonished and delighted that his 'paper' house was still standing. He would no doubt approve of the special membership scheme offered by the Friends of Strawberry Hill – donate £100 or more and you become a Dilettante, for £500 or more you become a Virtuoso, and for £1,000 or more you become a member of the Committee of Taste.

right View of the Turkish Boudoir, the one room in the original house that was completely changed by Lady Waldegrave in the 19th century.

left Walpole's medieval stained glass is a startling contrast to the Turkish embroidered ceiling.

name
   Simon Drake's House of Magic
address
   Secret location in central London
telephone
   020 7735 3434
website
   www.houseofmagic.co.uk
opening times
   Monthly public night: 7pm–1am
description
   Private residence and theatrical venue
original structure
   19th-century public house
interior
   Simon Drake, 1995 onwards
design style
   Victorian vaudeville meets Hammer House of Horror

above Close-up of the mirror in the Red Room.

opposite Entered via the Enchanted Garden, the first interior in the house is the Red Room, which at night glows with mirrors and candles.

His search for somewhere to live and to store a vast array of stage props led magician and illusionist Simon Drake to a disused, but once magnificent, pub – and ultimately to the alluring idea of a House of Magic. Originally he planned to create an entirely private residence, with domestic rooms upstairs and a highly original rehearsal space downstairs. The bars on the ground floor became the Red Room, the Auditorium and a third space featuring a 'Whispering Chair'. However, encouraged by friends and fellow performers, Drake began to realise that a slightly different use of the interior was possible, and today the theatrical areas of the building, collectively termed the Simon Drake House of Magic, are available either for exclusive hire or for the monthly ticketed public nights. Both house and owner provide a unique evening's entertainment.

The best way to get into the spirit of the House of Magic is to take up the suggestion of arriving by vintage taxi, blindfolded for the journey to the house's secret location. Guests are led into the Enchanted Garden that snakes around one side of the building, where the removal of blindfolds reveals cheeky Hammer House of Horror-style props alongside flamboyant pieces of architectural salvage. An astonishing spectacle in the midst of the hustle and bustle of London, this is the unique blend of Gothic humour and antique charm that is the House of Magic.

SIMON DRAKE'S HOUSE OF MAGIC

The first interior space is the gloriously gothic Red Room. Mirrors shimmer and candles flicker – you almost expect Christopher Lee to appear suddenly at the top of the stairs. Reflected in the burnished mirror are the Red Room's chandelier and the bejewelled mantelpiece, a riot of sparkling colour in the candlelight. A gilt clock sits amidst the candles and jewellery and, together with the mirror's extravagantly painted frame, creates a wonderful tableau of Gothic opulence.

Theatrical swags of curtain and Gothic woodwork are painted in a frolicking *trompe l'oeil.* A Pollock toy theatre and a pair of mechanical rabbits draped in

above Pillars, steps and a low wall separate the Red Room from the Auditorium. With gilt chairs and red curtaining, the view from the Red Room is reminiscent of an opera box.

right top The curious assembly of objects on the stage forms part of Simon Drake's magic show.

right Props from Simon's many shows are incorporated into the decor.

jewellery add to the sense of historical playfulness. At the foot of the stairs, the red walls and painted arches give way to flocked wallpaper, red roses up the banisters and a portrait on the wall. An ultraviolet light above the painting intermittently illuminates the grinning skull of the sitter. Nearby, a mirror emits a ghostly laugh if the frame is pressed. It's all zany fun in a crazy world.

Ranged along a low wall, gilt chairs in the Red Room face into the Auditorium. This was the back bar, and at the time of purchase 1840s mahogany and glass were still in situ. Local research revealed to Simon Drake that he had, quite by chance, chosen an area of London that had witnessed public entertainment of an

exuberance not unlike his own. The pub flourished when the Victorians flocked to the Surrey Gardens to see the phenomenally popular 'Mount Vesuvius'. This was a nightly dramatic enactment with a large painted backdrop, where a 1.5-hectare (3-acre) lake represented the Bay of Naples and fireworks created vivid 'eruption' special effects. Following drinks in the Red Room and dinner in the Auditorium (complete with deft entertainment from close-up tricksters), Simon Drake's show is also a fantastical crowd-pleaser – where illusions include gasp-inducing decapitations and amputations, lashings of special-effects blood, and mock horror from his glamorous (Gothic) assistants. A suit of armour, a huge rabbit's head and all manner of bizarre props form part of this 'magical extravaganza'.

It was in the Auditorium area that Drake noticed a solitary wrought-iron pillar

above Have your fortune told in the Whispering Chair, a *trompe l'oeil* extravaganza festooned with faux cobwebs.

above The Haunted Cellar provides a wonderful excuse to drape props with cobwebs and to rig up strange mechanical contraptions that startle the uninitiated.

that seemed to be of a later date. He is convinced – and there is illustrative evidence to support this – that it came from the Surrey Music Hall, an elaborate iron structure that was put up in the Surrey Gardens in 1856. Described at the time as London's 'largest, most commodious and most beautiful building, erected for public amusements, carnivals of wild beasts and wilder men', it held up to 12,000 people and had corner octagonal staircase towers topped with ornamental turrets. Destroyed by fire in 1861, it was rebuilt, but its days were numbered. The gardens were sold in 1877 for building development, and today a huge estate of housing plus a small park cover the site.

The Victorian-style entertainment continues with a visit to the Whispering Chair, where a disembodied voice tells your fortune, and to the Haunted Cellar, where Rafe the butler conducts you down a steep flight of low-ceilinged stairs. Coffins, skeletons and myriad props from film and stage (including *Sleuth* and *A Clockwork Orange*) are jumbled up in a glorious medley with flags from the Crimea and old coins and bottles that were all unearthed during building work. Back on the ground floor, the skeleton theme appears again in the ladies' lavatory.

Upstairs, the Drawing Room marks the first part of the domestic interior, although it is also open on public nights. Some of the older items in the room were restored or adapted with gusto by Drake. Examples include a fish tank that

left A place to relax on public nights, the Drawing Room is also Simon Drake's sitting room.

left The macabre and the theatrical meet in the corner of the Drawing Room.

left As part of the evening's entertainment, individual in-depth tarot readings are offered in the Egyptian Room.

above The shelves include books on levitation, the poetry of Blake, clowning and card tricks.

was formerly a cabinet for displaying jewellery, shutters that were made larger with old skirting board, and the chandelier, which arrived in thousands of bits and took hours to put together and wire up. Books and props, many from the US, complete the ensemble.

The Egyptian Room is the final element of the suite of rooms that forms the Simon Drake House of Magic. Used for tarot readings and as another quiet space, it is a surprise to step into such a vivid blue after the reds and ochres of the other rooms. Golden hieroglyphics and Egyptian symbols adorn the walls, while dark wooden cabinets house all manner of objects. Simon Drake describes the making of his House of Magic as an extremely satisfying creative experience. Since the Egyptian Room is also the bedroom, this is eccentric entertainment at its most cheeky and flamboyant.

name
   The Bath House
address
   Warwickshire, c/o Landmark Trust
telephone
   01628 825920 (Landmark Trust)
website
   www.landmarktrust.org.uk
description
   Holiday let
original structure
   Octagonal bath house in country
   estate, c. 1748
interior
   Landmark Trust, 1987–91
design style
   Shells and aquatic themes within
   Georgian elegance

Walk through the front door of the Bath House and you are met by a breath-taking vision of shell-work festoons, plaster icicles and a Georgian green-and-white colour scheme, all within an octagonal room with stunning countryside views. Formerly part of a large estate, the Bath House was a place of entertainment, providing a fashionable and exotic place to rest after a long walk, to enjoy the view, and to have picnics and tea parties. It was even the setting for a Victorian christening dinner. Now a highly unusual holiday let, this romantic and eccentric building can be yours – at least for a few days.

The Bath House was built in 1748 during the optimism of England's new Augustan age. Under the rule of Augustus, Rome's first emperor, the original Augustan age had been one of peaceful creativity after a period of civil war. In England, following the turbulent years of the 17th century, a movement grew to create a new golden age based on the glories of Augustan Rome. Thought to have been designed by the gentleman-architect Sanderson Miller, the Bath House can be understood as a boisterous embodiment of this spirit of Roman revival. It blends a playful throwback to the Roman baths (a grotto-like lower room) with the shell-festooned 18th-century elegance of the upper room.

above To the right of the bed is the door to the kitchen.

left The exquisitely recreated shell festoons are draped across all eight walls of the octagon, as they were in the 18th century.

opposite The upper room of the Bath House makes a unique and stylish open-plan holiday apartment.

THE BATH HOUSE

55

above Up above is the spectacular ceiling of plaster icicles. These were intended to convey an impression of the moment water drops turn into icicles.

As part of the fashion for locating exotic buildings in obscure parts of country estates, the Bath House was built for Sir Charles Mordaunt, 10th Baronet of Walton Hall. As can be seen in today's restoration, the main features of the upper room were the plaster icicles and the festoons of shell-work. The festoons appear at the top of all eight walls of the octagon. The use of shell decoration for the interior was the idea of Mary Delaney, whose sister lived nearby. Although better known for her paper flower pictures, Mary Delaney also excelled in shell-work. In 1754 she sent a barrel of shells to Walton, and probably supervised their arrangement.

The history of the Walton estate is one of plentiful wealth and leisure time followed by declining fortunes. After the Second World War, Walton Hall became a school and is now a luxury hotel, but the Bath House fell out of use and was vandalised. Eventually it was brought to the attention of the Landmark Trust, the charity that specialises in the rescue of small, but distinguished, historical buildings, and a lease was signed in 1987. By that time the vaulted ceiling had

fallen in, most of the plaster on the walls had gone, and all that remained of the festoons were marks where they once had been. Diana Reynell, well known for her meticulous work restoring shell grottos, undertook the recreation of the festoons. Survey drawings, old photographs and a few surviving shells helped in the restoration.

Restoring the Bath House to its flamboyant former glory took four years. Discoveries included old moulds for the plaster icicles under the floorboards, which were used to make new moulds for the replacement icicles. The central ceiling boss had vanished, so a new one was created. The chimney piece was also a new design. Its shell decoration echoes that of a chimney piece that was the work of either Mary Delaney or her sister. The stunning central rosette makes clever use of the few surviving 18th-century shells.

Part of the eccentric charm of the Bath House is that most of the living space is in this one room, containing bedroom, dining- and sitting-room furniture. The double bed with white bedspread is the perfect place from which to admire the gloriously restored ceiling, while the highly polished wooden furniture provides a dramatic contrast to the pale colour scheme. A large oak chest provides storage for extra bedding. This is not the place to bring large quantities of clothes – hanging space is restricted to a few hangers in a small space beside the staircase (accessed through a door to the left of the chimney piece). As with all Landmark Trust properties, the bookcase by the chimney piece contains titles appropriate to the building – such as *Seashells*, *Follies*, and *Trees and Shrubs of Britain*. A large and faded Persian-style carpet on the newly laid oak floor completes the feeling of historical cosiness. Meanwhile, neatly fitted into a small closet beside the door is the kitchen.

The staircase is revealing. Twisting upwards from the entrance level it is made of wood, newly inserted to take guests up to the bathroom. This final requirement of today's accommodation was ingeniously tucked into space above the entrance arch that frames the front door. On the wall beside the bathroom door

top Within the central rosette on the chimney-piece decoration are the few surviving 18th-century shells.

above The sitting-room area is based around the focal point of the chimney piece.

is an intriguing glass case displaying original fragments of the plasterwork in a way that is somehow reminiscent of Victorian displays of travel souvenirs. Written on the side are the words:

BATH HOUSE RESTORATION WALTON
PAINTED WALL FRAGMENTS
SHELLS FROM ORIGINAL FESTOONS (BRITISH ISLES AND WEST INDIES)
    WITH NEW SHELLS
WALL FRAGMENT WITH CUT-OUT FESTOON. ORIGINAL DESIGN FOR
    LEADWORK BOWS CARVED WOODEN CENTRE KNOT AND LEAD STRAPS
LATH AND PLASTER OF ORIGINAL WALL
ICICLE STALACTITES IN ORIGINAL AND NEW SETTINGS
LANDMARK TRUST 1991.

Twisting downwards from the entrance level is the original stone staircase (now with a handy rope for support). This leads down to the lower room, the eccentricity of which is announced by the most spectacular door. The lower room is the bath chamber, from which the building gets its name. Rough masonry overhead creates an extraordinary grotto effect, and suddenly the icicles of the upper room make more sense. The upper room represents the 18th-century, refined version of the rough antiquity of the lower room, with all its Roman connotations of function and form. The large, stone cold-water bath was the 18th-century cure for gout and other ailments, rather than being associated with regular cleanliness. The European 18th-century fashion for shell-work and grottos is well documented, but the effects of this fashion were rather more long-term than might be supposed. The French words 'rocaille' (the rockwork found in caves and grottos) and 'coquillage' (the shell-work used to adorn grotto walls, ceilings and floors) were the source of the word 'Rococo'. The term was coined around the turn of the 19th century and has remained a stylistic noun ever since.

below left At the top of the newly inserted portion of the staircase is this display cabinet featuring original plasterwork, shells and other materials.

below middle A closet opening off the main room provided space for the small, but skilfully designed, kitchen, with cupboards of all shapes and sizes fitted into the contours of the building.

below right This wonderfully exotic door, specially designed for the restoration, opens on to the stone floor that surrounds the bath chamber of the lower room.

With its pretensions of emulating ancient Roman architecture, yet being firmly rooted in the English tradition of country-estate landscaping, this extraordinary building is a wonderful example of English aristocratic eccentricity. Throughout the ages it has been the focus of a very English oddness, from those tea parties in a fantasy Classical paradise to the early 20th-century owners who left gravestones beside the Bath House marking the demise of much-loved pets. Today, the Landmark Trust logbook provides reassuring evidence that the English eccentric is alive and well. One delighted guest has written: 'It is possible to wake up and think one's a mermaid.'

right View of the bath chamber, with stone steps leading into the extremely cold water. Bathing was seen as a health cure. It had yet to be considered a leisure activity, or indeed an everyday hygienic necessity.

name
 Yew Tree Inn
address
 Cauldon, Staffordshire ST10 3EJ
telephone
 01538 308348
opening times
 Midday–2.30pm and 6pm–11pm
 (10.30pm on Sundays)
description
 Country pub stuffed full of antiques
original structure
 17th-century public house
interior
 Alan East, 1961 onwards
design style
 Antique shop that also serves
 excellent ale

Tucked away in the English countryside, one can still find 17th-century pubs, but the Yew Tree Inn in Staffordshire is quite unique. The huge old yew tree outside and attractive facade with its gables and mullioned windows do nothing to give the game away. The interior of this lovely old building is, however, quite astonishing.

Described by locals as one of the wonders of the Peak District, the inn is literally crammed with antiques and curiosities. A small lobby – on the right of which stand several large Victorian polyphons, and to the left of which is a closed-off room stuffed with all manner of objects – leads into the main area around the bar. A vista of dark wooden furniture opens up, with a cabinet housing Toby jugs, plates and other ceramics, and another cabinet that includes memorabilia such as a letter to the pub from a television crew. Amongst the wood, ceramics and silver, a mahogany gramophone with stunning green-flower horn stands proud, close to a sign for the rather cheaper Gallaher's Park Drive cigarettes at 2d for 10. Smokers today must read that sign with envy.

In the midst of all this, ordinary pub tables with beer mats and plastic ash trays are jumbled in with elegant antique seating. Every object has a story. Take, for instance, the four choir stalls set against the wall in the seating area to the left of the bar. They came from St Mary's Church, Stafford, and look completely at home in their new secular setting.

One of the many wonders of the Yew Tree Inn is that it sets you off on a world of discovery. Stumble across the pianola, with assorted music rolls precariously balanced on top, and suddenly you feel an urgent need to know exactly how it works (apparently it all depends on whether the music rolls were recorded by a pianist or simply perforated by a technician, using pencil marks that represented

above An amazing collection of antiques and curiosities is housed in this historic pub.

opposite A green cigarette sign provides a central focal feature to the area to the left of the bar.

YEW TREE INN

61

above In this seating area, choir stalls salvaged from a local church sit snugly beneath the low beams.

right At right angles to the piano is a pianola, with music rolls piled on top.

the original sheet music). This is more than a heap of antiques. It's a feast of popular culture, social history and good old-fashioned entertainment.

Continuing the theme of entertainment, the penny farthing leaning against the fireplace is a source of much discussion in the pub. Landlord and collector Alan East can tell you exactly the right point at which to get on it without falling off (since the rider's feet cannot reach the ground, the penny farthing is almost a unicycle). An English invention from 1870, its nickname came from the fact that the disparate wheel sizes reminded people of the large English penny and the smaller farthing. Victorian England would no doubt have loved the spectacle of a cyclist trying to stop suddenly, as this would often send the rider flying over the handlebars (known as a 'header'). Here at the Yew Tree Inn, however, as it gleams in its fireside setting surrounded by copper pans, the penny farthing looks deceptively harmless.

Antique seating is a continuous theme in this pub, and in the middle room is a splendid seat that came from the state drawing room at Alton Towers. Now a ruinous Gothic palace in the middle of the theme park and funfair, Alton was once a splendid Victorian mansion that gloried in the romanticism of the Gothic Revival (Augustus Welby Northmore Pugin, one of the movement's most influential figures, was involved in some of the decorative schemes). Set against the ancient walls of the inn, the seat's richly carved wood blends in seamlessly. Another Victorian mansion in the area, Hoar Cross Hall, was the original home of a highly

YEW TREE INN

above Many items in the pub originated from stately homes in the region, including this seat from Alton Towers.

opposite Featured on British television, the objects in this collectors' pub include a penny farthing bicycle positioned in the fireplace.

below The fireplace contains a wonderful collection of decorative ironwork, including a splendid fireguard.

decorative fire grate that spans the middle room's fireplace. Complete with old cooking pots and other highly collectable ironwork, the fireplace is a gloriously historic focal point.

Appropriately enough, the Yew Tree Inn contains many items of brewery advertising, ranging from metal plaques and posters to the attractive model entitled 'A Whitbread Dray, 1742'. It is amusing to notice that, rather than waste precious space with fancy seating arrangements, the driver sits on top of one of the barrels. Behind him an old poster advertises Gaymer's Olde English, billed as 'the original strong cyder'. While these objects are less surprising in an old established pub, it is unusual to find them positioned in front of an antique clock mechanism in a glass case. But then, this is a pub where the ring of the cash register takes you straight back in time.

Nestled beside packets of peanuts and bottles of spirits, this twinkling jewel of a cash register is a gorgeous throwback to the decorative Victorian and Edwardian approach to all things retail. The cash register is still fully operational, albeit in imperial currency – a minor detail for the owner, who simply ignores the old money signs. The ring is loud and clear, and the spring-loaded drawer still shoots out with considerable force. Up above, a copper kettle and the last-orders bell hang amidst a riot of glassware, tankards and the odd chamber pot.

On an upper floor, only accessible through the private, lived-in part of the pub,

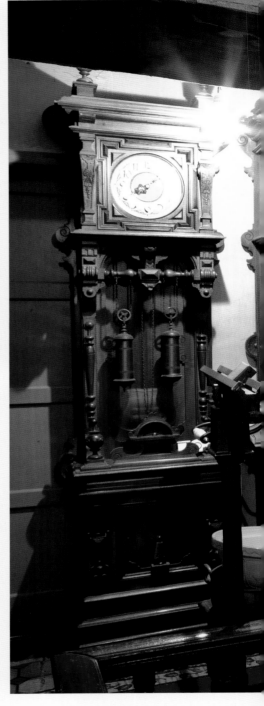

top Glasses and tankards hang above the bar, and monies are taken in an old imperial cash register.

above Clocks and pub-advertising ephemera can be found in every nook and cranny.

above Nestling in front of an upstairs window is a collection of wirelesses, gas lamps and other items.

above Beyond the wooden rocking horse are several musical long-case clocks.

lurk many more wonderful pieces of history, including a Jacobean four-poster bed, a Nestlé chocolate slot machine, Second World War helmets and a charming wooden rocking horse. An extremely impressive collection of musical long-case clocks is housed on this floor, as is an equally appealing collection of that timeless classic, the Bakelite wireless.

name
Rules Restaurant & Private Rooms
address
35 Maiden Lane, Covent Garden,
London WC2E 7LB
telephone
020 7836 5314
website
www.rules.co.uk
opening times
From midday every day of the week
(last orders: Monday to Saturday,
11:30pm; Sunday 10:30pm)
description
The oldest restaurant in London
original structure
18th-century terraced building
interior
Various, 1798 onwards
design style
The grouse season meets theatre
memorabilia

You might wonder at the name of this historic restaurant. Suggesting some form of rigid etiquette, the name is, in fact, simply that of its founder, Thomas Rule. Britain was 38 years into the reign of George III when Rule opened his restaurant in 1798. The Napoleonic Wars were in full swing; this was the year of Nelson's victory at the Battle of the Nile.

Rules continues to thrive at its original premises in Covent Garden. By the 18th century, Maiden Lane had developed from an ancient track to a busy commercial and residential street. In the 1720s, Voltaire lodged at a barbershop at number 21. JMW Turner was born at the same address in 1775, and 15 years later he moved with his father to number 26, where he painted *Fisherman at Sea*, his first exhibit at the Royal Academy. He was still resident in Maiden Lane when Rules opened at number 35.

The archives at Rules record that contemporary writers were soon praising the 'porter, pies and oysters' at the restaurant, and commenting on the 'rakes, dandies and superior intelligences who comprise its clientele'. With the Prince Regent in his prime, and that most famous of 18th-century dandies, Beau Brummel, having just quit the army for the bachelor lifestyle, times were good for rakes and dandies. As the years passed, Rules became a cherished part of the London scene. Its tables have been continually graced by writers, artists, lawyers, journalists and actors, not to mention several Princes of Wales. Former

opposite and above Suffused by the yellowish glow of the walls and lamps, the restaurant's individual areas of banquette seating are surrounded by a glorious mass of prints, photographs and paintings.

RULES RESTAURANT & PRIVATE ROOMS

opposite, top Dan Leno, the famous music-hall comedian, sits on high amongst the grouse and *Vanity Fair* prints in the Charles Dickens Room.

opposite, middle A curved corner shelf houses a full set of Dickens.

opposite, bottom The Charles Dickens Room can seat up to 12 diners.

left The Edwardian ceiling glass alludes to the performing arts. Beneath the glass are the following words: 'Many dancing dawns has this beauty seen/Her elegant curves obscured by smokey age/But this painted lady remembers theatre's dawn/And throws light upon all hands playing in linen fields.'

poet laureate John Betjeman described the ground floor of Rules as 'unique and irreplaceable, and part of literary and theatrical London'. Emphatically steeped in history, the interior is a charming expression of a quintessential English style.

The menu is particularly rich in game, mostly coming from Rules's own estate in the Pennines. Game dishes are offered all year round, by smoking the estate's surplus over oak chippings. (The kitchens get through 18,000 game birds a year, more than any other restaurant in Britain.) There is no danger, however, of the food being old-fashioned for modern palates, as there have been subtle changes to move with the times. Wild duck comes both roast and confit, gravy has

far left Game is an important part of both cuisine and decor at Rules.

left Located just within the entrance, this attractive fireplace is shown here dressed for Christmas.

become game jus. Meanwhile, the puddings are exquisitely hard to choose between, from warm sticky gingerbread with pear and vanilla compote and clotted cream, to bread-and-butter pudding with warm marmalade sauce.

Another relatively recent change has been the increased emphasis on private dining rooms, of which there are four, accessed via a creaky picture-lined staircase. On the first floor are the Charles Dickens Room and the King Edward VII Room. In the first of these, some of the memorabilia includes playbills for performances that Dickens produced and performed in, and that he brought to the restaurant himself. Like the restaurant downstairs, stuffed birds, playbills and *Vanity Fair* prints make up much of the room's character. Dickens' love of the theatre included a fascination with music-hall artists such as Dan Leno, whose bust sits amongst the grouse and champagne bottles. Surrounded by more feathered friends is a full set of Dickens.

Rather less predictable is the extraordinary whisky cabinet. A play on words becomes evident on the realisation that each whisky bottle is signed by a member of Margaret Thatcher's 1990 cabinet. Even more bizarrely, the bottle signed by the then Foreign Secretary Douglas Hurd was subsequently stolen. In its place is one signed by Tony Blair, causing many a wry smile about the policies

of the Labour leader. The restaurant's proximity to Whitehall makes it a popular haunt for politicians – one wonders what they make of the large 1997 painting of Margaret Thatcher in the restaurant.

It is for the theatre that this area of London is best known, and Rules has long been an unofficial 'green room' for the world of entertainment, from Henry Irving to Laurence Olivier. Amongst the many theatres that are a short walk from Rules is the Theatre Royal, Drury Lane. Famous royal mistress, Lillie Langtry, acted here. Rules was Edward VII's favourite place to wine and dine the beautiful actress, and a special curtain was installed so that they could discreetly slip up the stairs. Their favourite table by the window is now part of the King Edward VII Room.

above Entitled *The Thatcher Years*, John Spring's painting of 1997 dwarfs Max Wall, the Queen, and countless prints of lawyers and actors.

left The signatures of Tony Blair and Margaret Thatcher are seen in close proximity in the whisky cabinet.

RULES RESTAURANT & PRIVATE ROOMS

above View of the King Edward VII Room. Across the latticed windows of all the private dining rooms hang the same plush velvet curtains with antique gold tiebacks.

above right Two signed portraits of Edward VII and Lillie Langtry that have long hung on the walls at Rules were clearly the inspiration behind the impish cartoon that now shares the same wall.

below The performing arts are an integral part of the decor at Rules.

Amongst the fascinating items on the walls, two framed letters particularly stand out in this room. One is from Lillie Langtry's granddaughter, politely entreating Rules to spell her ancestor's name correctly, and the other is a wonderful anecdote, written in 1989 by the 87-year-old daughter of the chef at the time of Edward VII's visits. She describes how the king sent for her father to tell him that the sweet he had made was so beautiful it should have been under a glass vase.

Rules has two centuries of archival material, and much of it is on the walls. Up another floor is the John Betjeman Room, the newest of the private dining rooms. In 1971, when Rules was threatened by a demolition order as part of the proposed redevelopment of Covent Garden, John Betjeman spoke eloquently at the public inquiry, declaring: 'A place which has constantly been used by actors, managers and famous people, as Rules has, acquires an invisible atmosphere just as a church frequented by praying people acquires an atmosphere.' A full transcript of his words takes pride of place on the wall opposite the window.

The largest of the private rooms is the Greene Room. Named in honour of Graham Greene, it has the added benefit of being a delightful play on the theatrical connotations of the phrase. Although he spent much of his life in the south of France, Graham Greene came to Rules whenever he was in London, and always celebrated his birthday there. Featured on the fireplace are his words: 'There are some restaurants which give one a sense of being at home, more at home than in a friend's house, welcome, at peace. Rules in Maiden

THERE ARE SOME RESTAURANTS WHICH GIVE ONE A SENSE OF BEING AT HOME
MORE AT HOME THAN IN A FRIENDS HOUSE . . . . WELCOME . . . . AT PLACE . . . . .
RULES IN MAIDEN LANE WHERE I WENT FIRST MORE THAN 50 YEARS AGO
I EVEN PUT IT IN A NOVEL 'THE END OF THE AFFAIR' . . GRAHAM GREENE

opposite, top View of the John Betjeman Room, where petitions from countless diners line the walls above the picture rail in support of Betjeman's rallying of the troops to prevent demolition of the historic restaurant.

opposite, bottom Graham Greene was immensely fond of Rules, and the fireplace in the Greene Room includes his words to describe what the restaurant meant to him.

below The whisky chess set used in the 1959 film of *Our Man in Havana*, starring Alec Guinness and Maureen O'Hara. A rather fun *trompe l'oeil* effect creates a bookcase alongside the miniatures.

Lane, where I first went more than fifty years ago, is one. I even put it into a novel, *The End of the Affair*.'

The Greene Room is perhaps best known for a rather unique piece of Greene memorabilia. In *Our Man in Havana*, the hero secures the gun of the Chief of Police by getting him drunk during a chess game, in which a player taking a piece has to drink a miniature of whisky. Housed in a wooden glass-fronted cabinet are the miniatures that were used for the 1959 film of the book. They once belonged to Greene himself, and are displayed in true Rules style, in a cabinet surmounted by a clock, stuffed birds and champagne bottles.

On being told of the plan to name the room after him, the author wrote a charmingly modest letter, suggesting that the room should be named after his brother Hugh, as he, too, was a very regular diner. This type of personal rapport is the very fabric of Rules, forming an integral part of its decor as well as its reputation.

Graham Greene's Collection

In the book 'Our Man in Havana', James Wormold the hero secures the gun of the Chief of Police, Segura by getting him drunk during the game, in which a player taking a piece has to drink the miniature These miniatures belonging to Graham Greene, Co Starred in Carol Reed's 1959 film starring Alec Guinness and Maureen O'Hara

HISTORIC
ORIGINALITY

Stylish eccentricity is far from being the exclusive domain of today. Indeed, countless historical examples come to the fore when exploring the nature of eccentricity. The interiors in this section cover a broad range of historical styles, which all share a particular individuality. At Southside House in Wimbledon, centuries of family history coexist without any attempt at historical grouping or stylistic classification. It is a gloriously refreshing and authentic example of how a house can grow organically if left to develop naturally. Its eccentricity lies in its hotchpotch interior coupled with innumerable quirky details of family living. On a smaller scale, both in time and dimension, Charleston, in East Sussex, may be considered to have a similar organic and hotchpotch approach, but here the decorative styling was of a more cohesive nature. Colours may have faded and functions of rooms may have changed over the 60 years that it was inhabited by members of the Bloomsbury Group, but the key protagonists remained the same and consequently the style is reasonably constant throughout its history. It is the style itself, coupled with the antics of the group members, which make Charleston eccentrically original.

Stowe's Gothic Temple is a building with a very mixed past: from an architectural marvel featured in 18th-century guidebooks to a school armoury two centuries later, with all the attendant schoolboy wear and tear. Converted into Landmark Trust holiday accommodation in 1969, the original impact of this extraordinary building was brought back to life, and it still gleams for every new

HISTORIC

visitor. This is a building that falls into the intellectually knowing category of eccentricity – James Gibbs knew exactly what he was doing when he flouted the Classical conventions surrounding him. It was a clever building. To us the result is beautiful – to his peers it was astonishing.

A deliberate architectural flouting of convention also applies to both Beckford's Tower & Museum and Minterne House, but these two are typified by their use of a medley of styles. At the former, Henry Goodridge jumbled up revivalist styles to create a flamboyant showpiece for a demanding patron's priceless collection. While Goodridge was explaining that Beckford's tower combined the 'purity of Greek with the freedom of the Romanesque', Beckford seemed more concerned with extending its height, demanding the addition of a belvedere and still crying 'Higher!'. Half a century later, every area of established convention was being challenged, and the ensuing radicalism of the Arts and Crafts movement was itself reinvented in such unorthodox mixing of styles as the 1904 facades of Leonard Stokes's Minterne House in Dorset.

This is an architecture that is bending the rules, but it does so within a prescribed canon of possibilities. The uniqueness of Capesthorne Hall in Cheshire lies less in a premeditated sense of difference – although revivalism and historical individuality abound – and more in the combination of fate taking a hand coupled with a bold approach to the building today. A completely different interpretation of historical originality applies to Dennis Severs' house. Here nothing is left to chance. In the pursuit of a fleeting impression, everything is planned to the tiniest detail. This is a fastidious eccentricity that breaks new ground by being absolutely true to itself.

Ostentatious and bombastic, the invented family seat by Sir Merton Russell-Cotes puts the ego back in eccentric. Every gesture and every motif is about self-aggrandisement, and yet the resulting interior is less about power and more about an eccentric understanding of what makes art and design. This English eccentricity is a blustering one, not entirely sure of its facts, but not going to let anyone doubt its intention to impress. It is a far cry from the intellectualism of some of the historical properties in this chapter, but it remains irresistible nevertheless.

above Chaos reigns in the Smoking Room at Dennis Severs' House. Below panels of Spitalfields silk, snuff has been scattered all over the table, the empty bottles are piling up, and a wine glass has landed in a bowl of fruit.

ORIGINALITY

SUB ANCORA SPES

name
Southside House

address
3–4 Woodhayes Road, Wimbledon
Common, London SW19 4RJ

telephone
020 8946 7643

website
www.southsidehouse.com

opening times
March to October. Guided tours:
Wednesday, Saturday, Sunday
and bank holiday Monday (2pm,
3pm and 4pm)

description
Historical house with centuries of
family living

original structure
17th-century family house

interior
Various, from 17th century to 20th
century

design style:
Personally curated 'lived-in' look

The glorious eccentricity of this house lies in its indifference to any one period in history. The very old, the not quite so old and the very recent cohabit in a wonderful family jumble. The building is partly Restoration and partly Georgian, as well as being partly rebuilt after bombs hit it during the Second World War. What ties it all together is a very human story of generations patching up the building and adding their own possessions to the house.

Today the entrance is through the garden into a spacious, yet engaging, hall. School of Daniel Mytens (c. 1590–c. 1648) hangs alongside mid-20th-century art student (family member), while trunks, hat boxes, old toys and other bits and pieces that look as if they have just been brought down from the attic are piled up in the corners. The atmosphere is somehow familiar and warm, like a favourite baggy cardigan or a much-loved book. Evidently, Simon Jenkins felt the same when researching *England's Thousand Best Houses*: 'Everything is clearly in use,

opposite A corner of the garden
entrance hall beckons you into
the family house.

SOUTHSIDE HOUSE

above left Blocking the entire right-hand section of the bay window in the Breakfast Room is this haunting painting by James Sante entitled *Adversity*.

above right Family portraits from several generations adorn the Breakfast Room.

opposite, top 17th-century portraits peer through the spectacular chandelier.

opposite, left View of the Dining Room, looking towards the fireplace.

opposite, right The Jacobean fireplace, with portraits by Van Ravesteyn, is set off with colourful family items.

although whether by a Jane Austen heroine or a Hobbit is never quite clear.' He is writing here of the hall, but his comment could easily apply to the whole house.

Lurking in the dark Dutch Baroque style of the Breakfast Room is much evidence of the most recent three generations of the family. There is a portrait of Hilda Pennington-Mellor, daughter of the house, who in 1910 married Swedish author Dr Axel Munthe. Many visitors today are Swedish, keen to see the house and gardens where the author worked on revisions for *The Story of San Michele*. Their grandson Adam and his wife (painted in the 1980s) hang over the mantelpiece, which in turn is crammed with family photos and other memorabilia.

Yet in the same room that contains bottles of half-drunk vodka and whisky is an oil sketch by Constable. Alongside a 21st-birthday invitation to a 'Masked Brawl' are several paintings by Royal Academicians. Nothing is roped off, the wall hangings are sometimes stained, the Spanish leatherwork around the top of the walls peters out in places – this is not a house within which to stand on ceremony. Its charm lies in its immediacy and honesty.

Accessed via a small flight of steps, the full length of the Dining Room dramatically stretches out in front of you, culminating in lofty windows and heavy curtains. Eccentric touches include a Burne-Jones painting tucked into a room

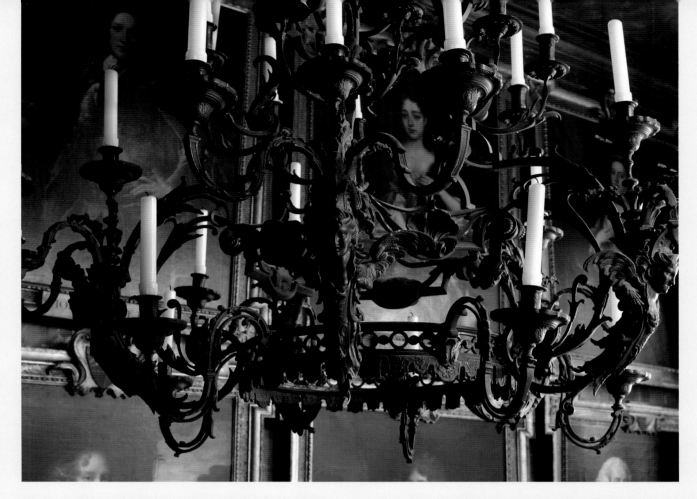

Sir Charles Kemeys Bar.

MARY Dau.r of Philip
Lord Wharton.

dominated by Van Dycks and a swag of plastic grapes draped across the Jacobean mantelpiece. A dappled ceiling arches over the room like a fabric canopy. Solid leather furniture, a splendidly long wooden table and a glorious chandelier by Daniel Marrow (designer of the William and Mary Hampton Court interiors) make this a truly fabulous room.

Up the stairs is the Library – a rather grand name for an extremely comfortable room stuffed with books that actually look as if they have been read. Old battered furniture and a Gainsborough covered with an old cloth to protect it from sunlight sit below busts on the shelves, and family photographs fill every available surface. Many of the photographs and objects in this room are connected to the world wars. During the Second World War, Malcolm, the younger son of Hilda Pennington-Mellor and Axel Munthe, was a volunteer in

above left General view of the Library, taken from behind the desk.

above right The naval cap worn in this photograph was recently found in the house.

opposite The main entrance hall was hit by bombing during the Second World War. Unable to afford major restoration, the family did much of the work themselves. The postwar rendition of the ceiling mural was perhaps the bravest undertaking.

below left View of the Prince of Wales Bedroom showing the bed with its huge fleur-de-lis motif.

below right The door of the Prince of Wales Bedroom was flamboyantly decorated in the 1940s by Peter, eldest son of Hilda Pennington-Mellor and Axel Munthe.

SOUTHSIDE HOUSE

Finland, escaped from German-occupied Norway, and then returned to organise Scandinavian resistance to Nazi occupation. He was eventually expelled from Sweden. Suffering from war wounds, he returned to Southside, painstakingly restoring parts of the house and creating a stage on which to present his family's history. His children now care for the house, through the Pennington-Mellor-Munthe Charity Trust.

Much of the house is Stuart, but rebuilding took place when the Hanoverian Frederick, Prince of Wales, was scheduled to visit, resulting in the hasty construction of the Prince of Wales Bedroom and the Music Room downstairs. The story goes that, shortly before the Prince's arrival, it was realised with horror that most portraits and decorative items in the house were distinctly Stuart. A maid was dispatched to make a judicious purchase – she returned with four cheap prints of various members of the royal family, which were slotted inside the mirror in the Prince of Wales Bedroom, where they remain to this day.

Displayed on the opposite wall to the bed is a cabinet of treasures, with handwritten labels (by Malcolm) introducing the valuable alongside the sentimental, the historically interesting mixed in with items made by members of the family when they were children. This hotchpotch of items is a charming example of the wonderful family jumble that so characterises this house.

The stately proportions of the Music Room – clearly two rooms knocked into one – create an elegant space looking out to the gardens. But as with so much

far left The 18th-century Music Room is still used for concerts, and is particularly attractive in the summer as it looks out on to the garden.

left Corner of the Music Room, with garden statuary seen through the window.

in the house, it is the family touches that make this room special. Lampshades are decorated with pasted-on sheets of drawings, there are quirky ornaments and piles of old sheet music, extraordinarily heavy-looking chandeliers are chained to the walls, and strategically placed sprigs of holly stop the visitor from sitting on delicate furniture. It was here that Lady Hamilton, Nelson's mistress, is said to have performed her famous 'attitudes'. Some years later, when she had fallen on hard times, the family bought the portrait of Romney from her that is now displayed in this room.

Next door is the Tapestry Room, which has survived today as an extraordinary time capsule. It is, in fact, hung with canvas, painted in the 18th-century to look like tapestry – common practice if one could not afford tapestry wall hangings. Unlike most houses, Southside was not adapted and updated in tune with changing fashions, and so the painted canvas is now an extremely rare survival. So, too, is the powder closet in the corner of the room, as once powdered wigs were no longer worn, the closets were usually dismantled to increase the size of the room. The glory of Southside is that generations of domestic life remain in situ.

above Front view of the powder closet, showing the tiny servant's door.

above Gentlemen would get their wigs powdered by leaning their head back into the hole and covering their faces with a cone. A servant sitting in the closet would then use bellows to blow powder over the wig.

right Detail of the painted canvas in the Tapestry Room.

name
Charleston
address
Firle, Lewes, East Sussex BN8 6LL
telephone
01323 811626
website
www.charleston.org.uk
opening times
July and August: Wednesdays to
Saturdays, 11.30am–6pm. March to
June, September and October:
Wednesdays to Sundays, 2pm to 6pm.
Entry is by guided tour only from
Wednesdays to Saturdays. Sundays
and Bank Holiday Mondays are
unguided.
description
Family home
original structure
Late Elizabethan
interior
Vanessa Bell, Duncan Grant and
others, 1916–1970s plus recent
restoration
design style
Colourful Post-Impressionist take on
Italian fresco

In a letter of 1919, Virginia Woolf wrote of her sister Vanessa's life at Charleston: 'Nessa presides over the most astonishing menage; Belgian hares, governesses, children, gardeners, hens, ducks and painting all the time, till every inch of the house is a different colour.' Although the Bloomsbury group of artists, writers and intellectuals were named after their London meetings, it is the country farmhouse to which Vanessa moved in 1916 that is now the best-known residence of the group. Charleston is the only surviving example of the domestic decorative work of artists Vanessa Bell and Duncan Grant. Flamboyant *trompe l'oeil* flowers, curvaceous nudes and mythical scenes decorate nearly every available surface, inspired by Italian fresco painting and the Post-Impressionists.

Accounts often refer euphemistically to the 'unconventional' household at Charleston. Accompanying Vanessa in 1916 were her two sons by former husband, art critic Clive Bell; her lover, Duncan Grant; and his lover, writer David Garnett. Many of the 'Bloomsberries' were either gay or bisexual, and they remained a tight-knit, exclusive group. Clive Bell, David Garnett and Maynard Keynes lived at Charleston for long periods of time, while Virginia and Leonard Woolf, EM Forster, Lytton Strachey and Roger Fry were frequent visitors.

Once Vanessa had negotiated a longer lease on the house, she was able to plan a purpose-built studio. Roger Fry, founder of the Omega Workshops, artist, critic and former lover of Vanessa, designed the large rectangular room that was built on the side of the house. It was a very cheap build, but the large space and long, high window created good working conditions. The Studio remains an amazing treasure trove of postcards and notes pinned to the mantelpiece, old inherited furniture mixed in with painted pieces, books, ceramics, photographs, brushes, tubes of paint, jars and, of course, numerous paintings.

above A cast of a 6th-century Chinese goddess of mercy (the original was once owned by Roger Fry) dominates the mantelpiece.

opposite The Studio fireplace has panels by Duncan from the early 1930s, while the tiles are a 1920s design of Vanessa's. The stove made this the warmest room in the house.

CHARLESTON

above left Housing various artists' materials, this cupboard's inner doors depict Adam and Eve. On top is a plaster-cast head that was rescued from the garden.

above In front of the mirror, a large jar sits atop a gramophone decorated by Vanessa in 1932.

left Contrasting strips of colour provide a lively backdrop to the works on the walls. The cast is of the ears of Michelangelo's David, and was acquired by Duncan from an art school.

A small L-shaped section contains stacked canvases alongside a cupboard with paintings of Adam and Eve by Duncan. The Studio was sometimes used for family theatricals, and this area was curtained off to make the wings. (Years later Vanessa created a studio in the attic, having decided to paint away from the constant interruptions on the ground floor.) Over on the opposite side of the Studio, the painted wall colours of soft pink, blue and grey can clearly be seen. In 1916 the house was quite dilapidated, and without electricity or central heating. After the First World War it was used only in the summer, but became a full-time home during the Second World War to escape the Blitz. Vanessa continued to live there for part of each year until her death in 1961. Duncan

above The room became Clive Bell's Study when he moved to Charleston at the outbreak of the Second World War.

right When the family first moved in, this was the sitting room. The windows were painted by Vanessa while the tiled table was Duncan's work.

struggled on into the 1970s, but eventually had to move out. The house is now maintained by the Charleston Trust. In its heyday, Charleston was a place of freedom, invention and creative endeavour. Above all, it was a family home where children grew up and played. Quentin Bell, Vanessa's younger son, writes charmingly of the damage done by him and his brother to various parts of the house as they boisterously played there in the summer holidays.

The room now known as Clive Bell's Study was for many years the family sitting room. The window area was the first part of the house to be decorated, in 1916–17, and was Vanessa's work. A few years later she painted the fire surround. Roger Fry designed the large blocks in front of the fireplace as an ingenious way to throw more heat into the room (the electric fire came later). To the left of the fireplace, a French antique chair is upholstered in a modern reproduction of a fabric design by Duncan; the fabric on the left-hand chair is a reproduction of a design by Vanessa. The room became Clive's study when he moved to Charleston in 1939.

Over the years, the Dining Room changed dramatically. A Victorian fire grate was removed to reveal a large, open hearth and, in 1939, Duncan, with the help of Quentin Bell, covered the existing layers of wallpaper with grey and yellow stencils on a black background. Not much care was taken over the durability of their work, and the walls in this room required extensive restoration. Another change was the installation of the telephone. Having divided opinion amongst the family, its presence was vindicated within days of its arrival when the fire brigade

below left The Dining Room hearth was created by Roger Fry in the mid-1920s.

below middle This view of the hallway from the dining room shows a 19th-century Chinese lacquered table and the Chinese god of earth.

had to be called to attend to a fire in the hall caused by an overheating stove.

Whilst the Studio is a quintessential Vanessa-and-Duncan workspace interior, the Garden Room shows their joint work within a living space. It was a popular room for relaxing on a summer's evening with the French windows thrown open. Early work includes Duncan's angels and musicians on the log box, and the figures above the fireplace that once carried a mirror (when it cracked, Duncan replaced it with the floral design still there today).

below On the Venetian side table are ceramics from the 1930s: the three soup bowls were made by Quentin Bell, the caddy was decorated by Angelica, and the plates and dishes were designed by Duncan for Clarice Cliff.

above Adding colour and charm to the fireplace, an 18th-century French ceramic lion seems to smile rather than roar.

right above A cast of a 1908 bust by Renoir faces a lamp stand decorated by Duncan in the 1920s.

right below In Duncan Grant's Bedroom is a lamp stand matching the one in the Garden Room.

opposite View towards the side window in the Garden Room. Beyond the fireplace is Vanessa's self-portrait.

Many years later, in the 1940s, Vanessa designed the grey-and-white stencilled paisley wallpaper for this room. This more sombre scheme reflected her mood at the time – in 1937 her eldest son Julian had been killed driving an ambulance in the Spanish Civil War, and in 1941 Virginia Woolf had committed suicide.

Dating from the early days are parts of Duncan Grant's Bedroom, painted by Vanessa. The doors and fireplace surround were painted in 1917. On Christmas day 1918, Vanessa gave birth to her daughter by Duncan in this room. The children grew up unaware that Angelica was not Clive's daughter, but it was well known amongst the Bloomsberries. Vanessa painted the distinctive window decoration in the latter half of the 1920s, and designed the window-seat cover in 1943. A cast of a Benin bronze sits on the window sill.

opposite The Library is a curious mix of the original scheme for Vanessa's bedroom (the door and the walls), and Clive's furniture and books.

above The painted door in this corner of Duncan Grant's Bedroom leads to a small dressing room. Above the mirror is *Tea Things*, painted by Vanessa in 1919.

Vanessa's bedroom was originally upstairs, in the room that is now the Library. The striking wall colour of black, with vertical bands of Venetian red in the corners, was her scheme for the bedroom. When Clive moved to Charleston in 1939, Vanessa moved downstairs so that he could relocate his library. The large bookcase, decorated by Duncan while it was still at Clive's London flat, sits beside the decorated door. The door panels, also by Duncan, date from early days at the house. A large portrait of Vanessa, painted by Duncan in 1942, hangs against the black wall and ensures that her presence is still very much a part of this room.

Something of the immensely engaging, eccentric Englishness of life at the farmhouse lives on. The Charleston Trust's website currently states: 'From time to time we gather in the kitchen at Charleston and stuff envelopes for a mailing, while chatting over tea and biscuits. This is a very sociable event, and an ideal way to start if you wish to volunteer on an occasional basis.' Vanessa could not have put it better herself.

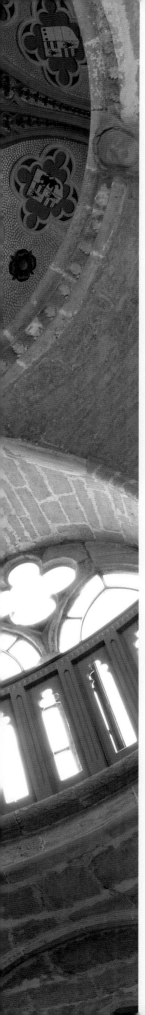

name
The Gothic Temple
address
Buckinghamshire, c/o Landmark Trust
telephone
01628 825920 (Landmark Trust)
website
www.landmarktrust.org.uk
description
Holiday let
original structure
Gothic Revival two-storey circular building with turrets, 1741
interior
Landmark Trust, 1970
design style
Rural idyll meets Gothic splendour

To some people Stowe is the name of an English public school; to others it conjures up images of a vast English country estate with spectacular landscaped gardens. The magnificent 18th-century Stowe House became the school in the 1920s, and today its buildings are being restored by the Stowe House Preservation Trust. Meanwhile, the landscaped gardens, with lakes, wooded valleys and more than 40 temples and monuments, are looked after by the National Trust. An exception to the rule in many ways, Stowe's Gothic Temple is administered by the Landmark Trust.

The 100-hectare (250-acre) estate is divided into five key areas. The Western Garden was created around 1720, with the intriguing theme of illicit and unrequited love. Based on the myth of Elysium, paradise for heroes of the gods, the Elysian Fields were begun in 1731. At the end of the decade, Hawkwell Field was incorporated into the gardens to become the Eastern Garden, a part of the estate where the boundaries between garden and nature were deliberately blurred. In the 1740s, Capability Brown's Grecian Valley came into being, becoming

opposite View from the ground floor into the vaulted ceiling. The painting of the ceiling was begun in 1747, and incorporates 54 shields bearing the arms of the Temple family.

above Detail of the vaulted ceiling. The building was sometimes referred to as the 'Temple of Ancestral Liberty'.

THE GOTHIC TEMPLE

IOI

left In this view, taken at gallery level, the Gothic windows of both floors can be seen. Painted in a new colour, the balustrade is original.

above Leading off the circular gallery are the two bedrooms, each snugly fitted into a tower.

opposite Sunlight streams through the windows onto the writing desk. The views are magnificent.

hugely influential on garden design throughout Britain and Europe. The fifth area was his South Vista, which remains the most idealised model of the English garden.

The Gothic Temple is located in the Eastern Garden, where all the buildings are by James Gibbs (the favourite architect of his employer, Richard Temple, 1st Lord Cobham). Built in 1741, drawing on medieval ecclesiastical sources, it was a startling departure from the Classicism that dominated the landscape at Stowe. A large triangular building of Northamptonshire ironstone, it has three circular towers attached to each point of the triangle, and a large circular space inside with a gallery. (It is not surprising to learn that Gibbs studied mathematics as part of his early training.) Stepping inside, the eye is immediately drawn upwards to the spectacular vaulted ceiling.

From the 1920s, the Temple was used by the school as an armoury. Restoration began in 1969, when the Landmark Trust took over the lease. The ceiling was carefully restored by Michael and Benjamin Gibbon in 1970.

The gallery is accessed by a stone spiral staircase that occupies one of the towers. At this level, curious and beautiful vistas open up where the circle-within-a-triangle device has left intriguing spaces in the three corners. These are put to attractive use with dark wooden furniture, such as a desk with ink stand or a wooden chest for storing linen. It is these touches that make the Gothic Temple feel homely rather than austere. The structure is based around three Gothic windows within arches that jut inwards and culminate in a corbel. Another three openings lead to the tower rooms.

Two of the towers house a bedroom each, below which are the kitchen and bathroom, respectively. The bedrooms are simple, circular rooms, just big enough for a double bed. With walls of a mustard yellow, both bedrooms share the same design of quatrefoil windows in stucco arches, white dado rail, and arch-shaped casement windows picked out in white. Gibbs's original design for the towers was one of blocked windows pierced only with small quatrefoil openings. For today's use, the least visible of these were fitted with simple metal-framed casements. Hanging space is provided by the inclusion of hat stands outside each bedroom.

Descending the spiral staircase to ground level once more, a big historical space is made cosy by groupings of sitting- and dining-room furniture, in much the same way as the Landmark Trust overcame the large octagonal space of the Bath House (see separate section). Here, too, there are faded Persian-style rugs, and the bookcase is well stocked with relevant and often quirky volumes.

right Unusual locations for the kitchen in Landmark Trust properties include a huge purpose-built wooden chest and small closet spaces – here at The Gothic Temple the circular kitchen seems quite large in comparison.

right The bathroom is located in the next tower along.

Curtains hang at the three large Gothic windows, and once again three openings lead into the tower rooms. On this floor, instead of vistas opening up, the spaces made by the circular towers abutting the inner triangle are cleverly utilised in the form of inbuilt storage cupboards. Crockery is stored by the kitchen; towels by the bathroom.

Architect Hugh Creighton designed the kitchen fittings to fit the circular room. The circular worktop is a neat solution, and the decorative mouldings and quatrefoil windows, repeated in the bedroom upstairs, make this an attractive and unusual design.

The deep, freestanding bath provides a splendid retreat if you want to be on your own for a while – rather like bathing in a church. In fact, in early guides the circular rooms in the towers were referred to as chapels. During a visit to Stowe in 1753, Horace Walpole wrote admiringly of the Gothic Temple in a letter to a fellow gentleman architect, John Chute, noting that: 'The windows are throughout consecrated with painted glass; most of it from the priory at Warwick.' Today, the building's only remaining coloured glass is in the bathroom.

The third tower houses the spiral staircase. Providing access to the gallery, the stairs also lead up to a belvedere. Stone seats and spectacular views invite a leisurely contemplation of Lord Cobham's fantasy landscape. The first recorded mention of the building was in 1742, in the revised 3rd edition of Daniel Defoe's *Tour through the Whole Island of Great Britain*. The entry is just as apposite today: 'A Gothick building, 70 feet high, presents itself on the Summit of a fine hill; which, we are told, is intended to be dedicated to Liberty.'

above left Close-up of the coloured glass in the bathroom.

above middle Highly appropriate in this countryside setting is the face on the front door. The wreath of acorn leaves and fir cones suggest that this is a depiction of the Green Man, seen on countless Gothic churches across Europe.

above A surprise for first-time visitors is that the spiral staircase provides access to three levels – the uppermost is outside.

opposite Firelight and candlelight sparkle in the highly polished copper and the glazes of porcelain in the kitchen.

left Fresh bread has just been cut.

name
Dennis Severs' House

address
18 Folgate Street, Spitalfields, London
E1 6BX

telephone
020 7247 4013

website
www.dennissevershouse.co.uk

opening times
Every Monday evening, except bank holidays (times vary according to season); first and third Sundays of the month (2pm–5pm); Mondays following the first and third Sundays of the month (midday–2pm)

description
Historical experience in a London townhouse

original structure
Brick terraced house, 1724

interior
Dennis Severs, 1979–99

design style
Eccentric take on 18th-century history to provoke the imagination

To visit Dennis Severs' House in his lifetime was an exhilarating experience. Severs' passionate desire was to create a 'still-life drama' out of his 18th-century merchant's house in London's Spitalfields. Aware that he was leaving himself open to criticism from design historians and lay visitors alike, he nevertheless persevered with an extraordinary belief in what the past can do to our imaginations today. Since his death in 1999, the house has been kept alive through the dedication of a uniquely skilled team and is brimful of atmosphere, leaving tantalising hints of what Severs had in mind. This is eccentricity at its most rewarding – entering his world, you cannot fail to be amazed and stimulated by what surrounds you.

Down the narrow, dark stairs, past a dimly lit cellar room, is the sudden glow of the kitchen. Far from being a gimmick, this is a house that asks you to look deep into the detail. For example, you might suddenly spot the child's shoes left under a chair, or a bread knife balanced precariously in a loaf. Someone has mischievously balanced gingerbread men amongst the china on the shelf above the fire, and a bonnet has been slung on the fireside chair. Severs wanted visitors to sense that the shape of the chair was the perfect fit for Rebecca the cook, his imaginary queen of the kitchen – but you don't need to know that. It is pleasing enough to notice that the chair is worn and snug and rounded.

above Through the basement window of the kitchen a birdcage motif can be seen on the tiles.

DENNIS SEVERS' HOUSE

For Severs, buying the house in 1979 after years of neglect, the kitchen was the first priority. This was to be his home, not a museum. Amazingly, the original dresser was still there, as were the sash windows with their thick glazing bars, the fireplace and the original lead plumbing. Penniless, but driven by an urge to recreate his childhood vision of England (when in his native California), in the early days he was forced to live off food abandoned in the local markets.

18 Folgate Street is a rare survival of the new merchant housing that appeared outside the city's walls in the early 1700s. Though running water was available to such households for just two hours a day at that time, the first incumbents would have been delighted at such luxury, which was afforded them by their own success. As you enter the dining room, a half-eaten apple is not yet browning, the wineglasses have finger marks on them and fruit cascades over

above The observant visitor will find a message from Dennis Severs pinned to the inside of the cupboard door.

opposite above In the dining room, canaries chatter noisily in birdcages in the window, a clock ticks and chimes, and the leftovers from a meal are on the table.

opposite below In her portrait, Mrs Gervais wears the cap that has been left on the chair.

the edge of a bowl. This is a stage-set with a difference – it lives. Bread and cakes are freshly baked, fruit is fresh, and the apple is bitten into just before visitors step in. Just as in Severs' time, visitors are invited to sense that the family has only just left the room. The dedication to preserve this intent is extraordinary, with the current staff attending to every detail with great care.

To create such an illusion, not only did Severs rig up recordings of voices, footsteps, street noise and so on, he also invented a family, regaling visitors with stories about Mr and Mrs Gervais and their children. In the dining room Mr Gervais' wig is left on a chair, while the right-hand alcove shows where the mistress of the house would retreat when her husband dined with friends. To the design historian the room is an eccentric jumble of eras, with chairs, wall colours, ceramics, glassware and portraits mixed together with abandon. Severs knew this and did not care. His interest in historical objects lay in capturing a glimpse of the lives of others. Many of the pieces are extremely valuable – the curtains of 1730s Spitalfields silk came from a country house (having been preserved in a chest) and the portrait of George III is by Zoffany – while others are of less value to a collector, but integral to the drama being played out here.

To emphasise the drama, the dining room contains the first of a number of notices. While the placing of objects was a careful signposting of domestic life, it seems there were moments when Severs was prompted to offer further explanation. Part of the notice reads:

… to pick up an object in a shop is a risk;
in a museum it is impossible;
in a Private House, particularly this one,
it is simply insensitive, numb to Mr
Severs' medium:
STILL LIFE DRAMA

You cannot help but admire his devotion to his cause.

Directly above this room is the drawing room, where it becomes clear that the family are passing through time as well as being just out of sight. The next generation have a more comfortable relationship with their wealth and status, and have changed their name to Jervis. Grinling Gibbons carvings ornament two sides of the room, while a circular tea-table draws the viewer into a feminine tableau. A pair of earrings lies abandoned next to the teapot and cups, and lumps of sugar spill onto the table. Over the elaborate gold-and-ivory mantelpiece, a portrait of the new Mrs Jervis surveys the drawing room.

above The drawing room is an elegant status symbol.

above A cup lies in pieces at the side of the chair, and a toasting fork has been abandoned before its pastry has had a chance to cook.

right Copious drinking and smoking led to hot debate in the masculine confines of the smoking room.

A cup lies broken on the floor; a house of cards has collapsed on a side table. These are the details visitors are meant to find. Look further, and one finds Dennis Severs the eccentric at work. The gilt borders on the window panelling stop when out of view behind the curtains, and the chimneypiece is proportionally too short for the room (to enable the portrait to fit). But does it matter? In his book about the house, *18 Folgate Street: The Tale of a House in Spitalfields*, Severs wrote: 'I began working on this room one evening in late October 1979. As in the other rooms, I began searching for clues as to what to do. I was not looking for clues to restoration, but more to reincarnation.' Beneath painted and wallpapered board lay the original panelling, and externally the three windows had been embellished with ornamental fretwork. Severs responded with this stately interior.

Next to the drawing room is the smoking room, which began as homage to the London coffeehouse so often depicted in 18th-century engravings. But when Severs bought a Hogarth and placed it over the fireplace, the room suddenly took on a new role – to recreate the aftermath of the drunken scene in the painting.

DENNIS SEVERS' HOUSE

Details such as the blue-and-white punch bowl, the knocked-over chair and the spilt red wine are obvious. Less so, perhaps, are the coat slung to one side that is also worn in the picture, the snuff spilled all over a side table, the abandoned wig, the fruit peelings and the broken glass thrown into the ashes in the hearth. This small room is a triumph of imagination.

The floor above boasts the bedchamber of the next generation down, at the end of the Georgian era. (The Regency happens in the boudoir next door.)

above Detail of the mantelpiece, with all its ephemera from the night before.

DENNIS SEVERS' HOUSE

Delicate pastels and the vogue for chinoiserie dominate here, but the extraordinary chimney piece of blue-and-white china would never have been found in a bedroom of this period. The eccentric Severs delighted in mixing historical aesthetics with his own. Relishing the theatre of his history, he would push the unsuspecting visitor behind the bedroom screen as voices approached to create a sense of hiding until the danger of being discovered had passed. He would be thrilled to know that 18 Folgate Street is alive and well.

above left A large four-poster dominates the bedroom, with rumpled sheets and a used chamber pot beside it.

above Breakfast has just been consumed in front of the elaborate chimneypiece.

name	description
Beckford's Tower & Museum	Museum, plus holiday let on ground floor
address	original structure
Lansdown Road, Bath BA1 9BH	Private retreat in the form of a tower, 1827
telephone	interior
01225 460705 (Bath Preservation Trust)/01628 825920 (Landmark Trust)	Bath Preservation Trust and Landmark Trust, 2001
website	design style
www.bath-preservation-trust.org.uk/ www.landmarktrust.org.uk	Displays of exuberance
opening times	
Museum: Easter to end October, weekends and bank holiday Mondays, 10.30am to 5pm	

Born into enormous wealth, William Beckford is perhaps best known today for Fonthill Abbey, his great neo-Gothic house built by James Wyatt in 1796. (A few sections of the building survive in the park near Fonthill Gifford in Wiltshire.) During his youth, Beckford was ostracised by polite society, dubbed 'the fool of Fonthill', and refused a peerage. The reason for this was his homosexual lifestyle. In his later years he replaced scandalous hedonism with respectable eccentricity, and at the age of 62 he moved to Bath. He purchased the land behind his home in Lansdown Crescent and created a mile-long route through landscaped gardens to the top of Lansdown Hill, where he built the 36-metre (120-foot) Greco-Italian tower now known as Beckford's Tower.

Designed by innovative Bath architect Henry Goodridge and begun in 1826, the tower was constructed to house the most important works of art and books in Beckford's extensive collections. According to Goodridge's son, Beckford was not satisfied with the original design once built, demanding that a belvedere be added to the top. Recently restored by the Bath Preservation Trust with support from the Heritage Lottery Fund, this astonishing room can once more be visited by climbing the tower's dramatic cantilevered staircase of 156 steps.

above View of the belvedere.

opposite Looking down the tower staircase.

BECKFORD'S TOWER & MUSEUM

117

Each morning, accompanied by his dwarf and pack of spaniels, Beckford would ride to his sumptuous tower to read, write and contemplate his treasures. From his beloved belvedere he had views as far as Fonthill in Wiltshire and across the Bristol Channel to Wales. Hanging at the plate-glass sash windows are eight floor-length damask curtains that, along with the bronze curtain rail, were especially commissioned as part of the recent restoration. The spectacularly ornate plaster ceiling was the only one in the tower to remain intact. The top layer of coffers and egg and dart, which had been destroyed in earlier repair works, has been reinstated. Above the belvedere is a gilded octagonal lantern, added to satisfy Beckford's desire for yet more height and drama. A wooden staircase to the very top was enclosed in a drum in the centre of the belvedere, now recreated in a marbled oilcloth. Reproduction stools with scarlet leather and fringing complete the room.

Combining Greek Revival with neo-Medievalism, the tower was an eccentric and extraordinary build. Servants who guarded the collection slept in the single-storey projection on the ground floor. The rest of the tower was essentially a stone cube with opulent, but cabinet-sized, rooms designed purely for the display of objects. There was no bedroom, kitchen or dining room.

above In the museum, Beckford's huge marble console sits in front of the unmistakable windows of his tower.

Sadly, none of the interior decor on the first floor survived a fire in 1931, and this floor now houses the museum. Furniture originally made for the tower is exhibited alongside paintings, prints and other objects illustrating Beckford's life, thus continuing the original function of the rooms.

On Beckford's death, in 1844, the tower and gardens were sold to a Bath publican. Horrified, Beckford's daughter bought them back and passed them to the rector of Walcot parish. The tower became a funerary chapel and the gardens a cemetery. Deemed redundant in 1969, the tower was bought by a local couple, Elizabeth and Leslie Hilliard, who converted the single-storey projection on the ground floor into an apartment. In 1977 they set up the Beckford Tower Trust and opened the tower to the public. Since 1993, it has been owned by the Bath Preservation Trust and administered by the Beckford Tower Trust, and in 2000 the Landmark Trust was invited to convert the ground floor into a holiday apartment. The original layout for this floor included a dark, windowless Vestibule beside the rich and dazzling Scarlet Drawing Room. The initial Landmark Trust planning was based around the restoration of the partition wall. However, most unusually for the trust, the decision was then taken to recreate the two spaces as closely as possible to Beckford's original. The result is a stupendous and ingenious reincarnation of an enthralling interior.

below On the floor below the museum, the apartment kitchen features its own version of the console, in wood.

So unobtrusive are the fixtures and fittings in the kitchen that it is easy to mistake it for a corridor – albeit a very elegant one. Using all the decorative elements of Beckford's Vestibule, the space once more runs the full length of the drawing room to its right. Paint replaces the wall coverings of the original, and a stone effect is painted on the wooden pilasters and mirror surround. The sink and cooker hob are sunk into a black work surface, against black tiles set below red wall cupboards matching the red of the walls. Cupboards at floor level are painted in the same stone effect as the pilasters, as is the radiator. The presence of a recessed cupboard on the opposite wall is made obvious only by two small holes for opening (thus avoiding obtrusive handles).

The elegant console table on the left is actually made of wood, with inbuilt drawers for cutlery and kitchen utensils, and a sturdy glass top. On the floor above, in the museum, sits the original marble pier-table on which the console is based. The original was only recently acquired by the museum, completing a fascinating exchange between old and new that Beckford would have rather enjoyed. Paintings show that the table was positioned in the same place in the

above Close-up of the coffered ceiling in the Scarlet Drawing Room.

below The Scarlet Drawing Room, now the living room of the Landmark Trust apartment.

BECKFORD'S TOWER & MUSEUM

above View of the window area, with a copy of a circular table in the museum.

below The bathroom makes clever use of space, and is dominated by the round-arched window.

Vestibule as the console is today. The long, dark kitchen creates a vista not untypical of a Victorian vestibule full of treasures, culminating in a massive rounded door. All the doors in the apartment are based on an original door that now opens into the bathroom.

The showstopper in the apartment is, just as its predecessor was, the Scarlet Drawing Room. The space underwent a number of changes after Beckford's death. A single-storey chapel from 1848 to 1931, it became a two-storey chapel in 1934, before serving as a living room for the Hilliards from 1971 to 1977. Now the plaster mouldings have been reinstated, floor-length curtains hung, and a specially commissioned carpet laid that imitates Beckford's original (red with black quatrefoils). The silk-like scarlet wall coverings are, in fact, cotton moire with a watermarked sheen. The radiators are painted red to recede into the wall colour, while the theatrically inspired coffered-effect ceiling is a magnificent tribute to Beckford's sumptuous ceilings.

Other attractive touches include wooden urns containing concealed uplighting, the Landmark Trust trademark of well-stocked bookcases, and oil paintings with large gilt frames. The circular table in the window area is a copy of a table that, according to contemporary images, was located in the same position. Again, the original is in the museum. The 1930s steel-casement windows have been kept as they are, as they are close in appearance to the plate-glass originals. In time, however, the Landmark Trust plans to return the windows to plate glass and gilded-iron grilles.

The two bedrooms for the apartment, referred to as the North Bedroom and South Bedroom, are located in the former servants' quarters, while the bathroom is in a space believed to have been the well pumphouse. Here, the fittings are arranged carefully; for example, the bath is inserted snugly beneath the window sill. This room has been left deliberately simple, allowing the original features to be part of the decorative scheme.

Brought back to life after serious neglect for much of the 20th century, today the tower is a wonderful example of how restoration and informed re-creation can coexist successfully. The tower was designed to dazzle Beckford's visitors as well as to showcase his collections, and the spirit of the building lives once more in the restored belvedere and the evocative apartment on the ground floor. Future plans involve further restoration on other floors, as well as the inevitable ongoing programme of exterior conservation resulting from the exposed position of the building. Presenting a striking silhouette on the skyline, its gilt lantern glinting in the sunlight, the tower is a fitting memorial to Beckford's achievements.

name
Russell-Cotes Art Gallery & Museum
address
East Cliff, Bournemouth, Dorset BH1 3AA
telephone
01202 451800
website
www.russell-cotes.bournemouth.gov.uk
opening times
Tuesday to Sunday: 10am–5pm

description
Family home built with its future role as a museum in mind
original structure
Showpiece house, 1901
interior
Various
design style
An ostentatious mix of architectural styles

Merton and Annie Russell-Cotes embarked on an upwardly mobile lifestyle when Annie inherited her father's cotton-spinning fortune in 1877. Their home and business had been the Bath Hotel. It now became the extremely profitable Royal Bath Hotel, filled with contemporary British art as well as souvenirs and artefacts from several tours around the world. In 1894 Merton became Mayor of Bournemouth, and three years later he was knighted. In that same year, plans were drawn up for a brand new 'ancestral' home. East Cliff Hall was to be both family seat and showcase for the couple's growing collections.

Unusually, the house was always intended to become a museum. In the 1880s the Russell-Cotes had sent large sections of their collection on tour, to galleries throughout Britain, and in 1908 they gave East Cliff Hall to the Bournemouth Corporation as a museum and art gallery, on the proviso that they could live there until they died. (During their lifetime, members of the public could obtain tickets for admission on Wednesday afternoons.)

Construction of East Cliff Hall began in 1898. The architect was the little-known John Frederick Fogerty, who had to tolerate such declarations as: 'I had made up my mind to construct it architecturally to combine the Renaissance with Italian and old Scottish Baronial styles' from Merton Russell-Cotes (who recalled those early days in his autobiography, privately printed in 1921). The interior is dominated by a large top-lit central hall, which

above The night sky, complete with bat, owl and comet, is depicted in the stained-glass dome over the main staircase.

opposite In the 1900s, the gallery rails were used to display Maori cloaks and animal skins. Recent restoration does not include a revival of this practice.

below Surrounding this rather saucy bather are huge Victorian paintings of biblical scenes and (male) celebrities of the day.

RUSSELL-COTES ART GALLERY & MUSEUM

123

above left Recently cleaned, John Thomas's peacock paintings in the Dining Room glow once more against the magnificent red of the imitation-leather wall coverings.

above right Various components of these chandeliers lay neglected in the attic for many years.

opposite Marble bust of John Landseer, dating from 1882. John Landseer was an engraver who fathered a highly artistic family – including Edwin (later Sir Edwin), famous for his paintings of horses, dogs, lions and stags.

was always filled with a bizarre assortment of objects and a great number of paintings on the walls.

The main staircase, complete with stained-glass dome, is a riot of bright colour and bold decoration. In a golden niche above the staircase is *The Bathers*, an unattributed sculpture from the late 19th century. A note within the correspondence of Norman Silvester (curator from 1931 to 1959) indicates that not everyone was impressed by this piece. The disapproval is palpable: 'Marble is not a suitable medium upon which to portray the intricacy of the knitted garment.' Russell-Cotes, however, showed considerable enthusiasm for depictions of attractive women, and they form one of the principal themes of his collection.

The rich decoration of the hall was already out of date by the time it was being executed, but it provides an opulent backdrop to the bust of Sir Edwin Landseer's father, depicted posthumously in the cravat and stiff collar of early

Victorians. The blue-and-white china above the door behind him, so popular in the 19th century, appears again in the Dining Room. This was the principal room on the ground floor, and features peacocks and fruit lavishly painted by John Thomas. Both he and his son Oliver had decorated the Bath Hotel, and at East Cliff Hall their work can be seen in nearly every room. Some of it is pretty poor, but it is an integral part of what makes this building unique and rather fun. A mixture of styles is very evident here, with a Tudor-style ceiling and an Elizabethan-style inglenook fireplace.

The function and style of several of the rooms upstairs changed during the years in which the house was inhabited. The Mikado Room, for example, began as the Blue Room, a bedroom often used by the Russell-Cotes' granddaughter. On Annie Cotes' death in 1920, Sir Russell-Cotes dedicated this room to her memory by converting it into a display of objects they had brought back from Japan in 1885. These comprised a curious assembly of old and new, cheap and

above Reading the dedication in the Mikado Room, it might be considered churlish to think of the financial advantages of Merton's marriage to Annie.

below These unlabelled objects in the Mikado Room were mostly brought back from the couple's extensive tour of Japan in 1885.

Oliver Thomas (son of John) used photographs of the Emperor and Empress Meiji that had been presented to the Russell-Cotes while in Japan as his source material for the coving paintings.

highly valuable, and included assorted Noh masks and a magnificent Buddhist shrine. The Russell-Cotes' collecting seems to have involved a scattergun approach, thereby obtaining all manner of good and not-so-good objects. They left no records of provenance.

To convert the bedroom to its new role, the blue walls were painted over in a rich red, the joinery was painted black, and the fireplace was removed. Fittingly, the room overlooks the Japanese Garden. The clifftop garden was recently restored to its original 1921 design as part of a major Heritage Lottery Fund refurbishment project, which also involved work on the fabric of the building, a faithful restoration of the unique historic interiors, and improved visitor services.

The Red Room was originally Russell-Cotes' bedroom, and has Venus and other 'heavenly beauties' painted on the ceiling. Rather more enthralling, however, is the Moorish Alcove. Another tribute to travels abroad (the Russell-Cotes visited the Alhambra in 1910), it is actually based on designs that were featured in Owen Jones's *The Grammar of Ornament*, the essential Victorian-design sourcebook. Taken from Owen Jones is a repeated motif of Arabic script around the edge of the dome that reads: 'There is no victor but God.' Originally three doors opened into this area, but these were removed when the house opened as a museum in 1922.

Lest we forget Merton Russell-Cotes' very considerable desire to move up

through the social ranks, the Study is full of references to his efforts in this field. Over the doors are carved heraldic shields, while the fireplace is lined with tiles that depict his monogram and coat-of-arms. The Tynecastle wallpaper is actually embossed flax. The frieze, also Tynecastle, includes the fleur-de-lis, English rose and Scottish thistle in its design. Some of the paintings in this room are of the slightly risqué nature that was kept to the male confines of a study.

The former Library, next to the Study, was converted to a room dedicated to Russell-Cotes' good friend, actor Sir Henry Irving. Sir Merton and his son Herbert

above The painting around the bust of Sir Henry Irving was covered over in the 1950s when the room was painted pink – thankfully all is now restored to its former theatricality.

right As in the Study, coat-of-arms tiles appear in the fireplace that dominates the Morning Room downstairs.

opposite Cupids, mythical sea creatures, monkeys and a winged horse add to the swirling mass of figures on the ceiling of the Morning Room.

bought many of the actor's personal effects after his death, including his stage make-up box, a bag and girdle worn by Ellen Terry as Lady Macbeth, numerous autographed items such as postcards and playbills, and the human skull that Irving used in performances of *Hamlet*. Scenes from plays that Irving made his own were pasted to the ceiling by Oliver Thomas, and the walls were painted brown.

In the Morning Room, a surprise lurks up above. The fantastical ceiling was painted in 1949 by Scottish artist Anna Zinkeisen, who is perhaps best known for painting murals, along with her sister Doris, for the liner Queen Mary. Women with diaphanous drapes cavort with various creatures, and chariots and columns add to the mythological fantasy. Perched on top of the cliffs, East Cliff Hall was most certainly an architectural fantasy, and its charming ostentation continues to amaze and enthral.

name
Capesthorne Hall
address
Siddington, Macclesfield, Cheshire
SK11 9JY
telephone
01625 861221
website
www.capesthorne.com
opening times
April to October: Sundays,
Wednesdays and bank holidays. (Hall
open 1.30pm–4.00pm)
description
Country house and estate
original structure
Neo-Jacobean house of 1837 and
1862
interior
Various
design style
Neo-Jacobean flamboyance mixed
with modern family life

opposite View of the *Winter* mural in the little
theatre at Capesthorne Hall. Damp has been a
constant battle.

Without a matchstick man or a factory chimney in sight, LS Lowry painted a view
of Capesthorne Hall in 1954. The hall's flamboyant red-brick turrets, central
arcading and flanking wings adorn the crest of a gentle green slope, while the
river dominates the foreground. Although he is best remembered for industrial
scenes, Lowry painted many images of historical buildings and countryside
views. He moved to Cheshire in the 1940s, not far from Capesthorne, and was
no doubt attracted by the hall's striking silhouette and strong colours.

The building Lowry painted, and that which we see today, is a fascinating
example of two architects working within the same style, but in their own
individual ways. In 1837 Edward Blore began a major remodelling of the house,
at the behest of the new squire (who had already upset the apple cart by
opposing the family's traditional Tory stance to become a Whig MP). Blore's
extensive changes were based on a neo-Jacobean style. Interested in the
architecture of Scottish castles, his remodelling included the distinctive turrets
and pinnacles. However, in 1861 fire gutted the entire central section, with the
two wings saved only by a change in wind direction. Anthony Salvin, widely
known for his exuberant merging of Gothic, Jacobethan and Baroque styles at

CAPESTHORNE
HALL

Harlaxton Manor in Lincolnshire, was appointed to rebuild the hall. Salvin continued the neo-Jacobean, but converted the three storeys into two and gave the main rooms excessively high ceilings and ornate decoration.

Not only is the hall a glorious mix of two architects indulging their revivalist fantasies, it also remains a fascinating and welcoming family home. Today weddings, craft fairs and regular open days to the public somehow manage to keep it ticking over. In its heyday, cars driving up the spectacular vista would have belonged to guests, many of whom came to stay for a relaxing weekend in

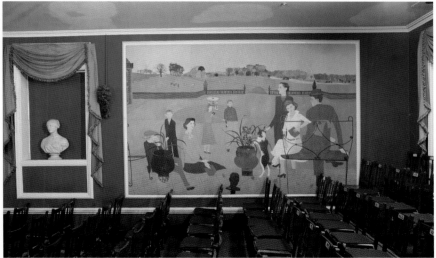

the country – but instead found themselves caught up in family activities such as the 'Capesthorne theatricals'. These were taken extremely seriously and, indeed, one family member went on to become a professional actor. In 1890 part of the stable block had been converted to a little theatre. Just inside the entrance to the auditorium is *Winter*, the last vestige of the original decorative scheme. The auditorium is crowned by a splendid ceiling of white clouds and blue sky, while deep-blue walls surround a striking series of later murals that continues the theme of the four seasons.

Painted in 1953 by Eric Ritchie, these murals were commissioned in memory of Kitty Brownlow, a member of the family who had encouraged the revival of the theatricals after the First World War, and became the *tour de force* behind the theatricals until the 1950s. *Autumn* is a family portrait, overlooking the rolling Cheshire countryside.

During the Second World War, Capesthorne was used as a Red Cross hospital, and ENSA actors entertained the troops here. It is still fully operational as a theatre, but nowadays is more often used for conferences.

above The wonderfully painted safety curtain remains in situ in the auditorium.

left In *Spring*, Kitty Brownlow is 'the bride', with the unmistakable red turrets of Capesthorne in the background.

above right In *Autumn*, the present squire appears as a boy, Kitty Brownlow is seated on the bench, and her late husband is represented by the bust in the foreground.

Today, William Bromley Davenport (Lord Lieutenant of Cheshire) and his American wife Elizabeth (a professional artist), are the latest of eight generations at Capesthorne Hall. Elizabeth is responsible for a number of new decorative schemes, especially on the ground floor. Blore's original entrance hall remains much the same as it was in the 1840s, except that the walls are now a strong yellow colour. The Jacobeans would have used bright colour for their interiors, so why not? This continues into the Sculpture Gallery, which leads to the main staircase, designed by Salvin.

A key room on the ground floor is the Queen Anne Room, which to previous generations was known as the State Dining Room. In those days it had displays of costume and silverware. The present Mrs Bromley-Davenport decided to lighten and brighten the space, taking as her colour scheme an apple green and a salmon pink from the Coalport porcelain displayed in the turret alcoves. The striking rope-design curtains are of a 1960s fabric by Hungarian-born, British-based textile designer Michael Szell (who was responsible for the redecoration of the throne room at Windsor Castle).

Inevitably, a house with many centuries of history has accumulated a huge assortment of objects, some worth a great deal of money and others equally valuable from a social-history perspective. Upstairs at Capesthorne, some of the

right The alcoves in the Queen Anne Room are set into the circular turrets of Blore's neo-Jacobean remodelling.

opposite, top Behind the central staircase, the passageway culminates in a charming painting of family members in the Library.

opposite, middle The yellow walls provide a bold backdrop for the marble antiquities and casts that were a prerequisite for any self-respecting country house. Here, one of a pair of casts of Canova's *Dancing Girls* flanks the entrance to the Saloon.

opposite, bottom Viewed through the spectacular hall mirror, family portraits can be seen on the walls above Salvin's staircase.

right The monumental fireplace and heraldic mantelpiece in the Queen Anne Room is framed by the apple green of the new decorative scheme.

bedrooms have been used for charming themed displays. The first of these is the Children's Room. 20th-century wallpaper, a made-up bed and an en-suite bathroom are reminders that this is a home, but what paying visitors see is an enchanting display of wooden toys and children's clothing that were once played with, and worn by, various members of the family.

Another fun little room is the Box Room, so named for its splendid collection of boxes of all shapes and sizes, from all over the house, and dating from many different eras. The curtains were once a beautiful white tablecloth, and now hang against gentle blue walls. The blue-and-white theme is engagingly concluded with the display of plates around the mirror. Hat boxes, medicine chests, a portable writing desk, a cabinet with intricate inlay, an early record player, travel games, little trinket boxes and battered box-style suitcases present a wonderful array of wood

above Amongst these classic toys is a wooden truck bearing the B-D initials of the Bromley-Davenport family. Shoes, coat, hat and gloves worn by the present squire as a child grace an armchair in the corner.

opposite Items in the Box Room, a former dressing room, were hung and positioned by the butler. Having worked for more than 40 years at the house, he and his wife are an integral part of life at Capesthorne.

and leather against the rich browns of the marble fireplace and polished floor.

The present squire's father was born in the Tower Room in 1903. He spent his early married life living in the Nursery Wing, and then inherited Capesthorne on the death of his bachelor uncle. Like his son after him, he married an American, who brought antiques, books, china and furniture to the hall. It was decided to house this collection in the sympathetic context of a carefully recreated American Room, and the result is rather astonishing. The atmosphere here is entirely distinct from the neo-Jacobean house that surrounds it. The furniture is the creation of 18th-century American cabinetmakers, and the china was made in England for the colonial market. In the corner, by the window, is a grandfather clock that stood on the staircase of a Philadelphia home for many years, chiming out the hours for Quaker meetings. Family photographs are dotted about, a panel

CAPESTHORNE HALL

of woven linen commemorates the Declaration of Independence, and samplers and prints adorn the walls. The American tester bed dates from about 1790 and came from Boston; it originally belonged to the well-known Lodge family.

At Capesthorne Hall, wonderful visual monuments to the quintessential English-country-house lifestyle, such as the theatre, exist alongside the present owners' infectious warmth and obvious delight in the hall's interiors. This is not a clinical stately home, grudgingly opening its doors to the public and making grandiose statements about the glories of the past as opposed to the horrors of society today. It is the home of a family who take care of a historic building, but are not afraid to embrace such modern notions as commercial enterprise and contemporary design. Laudably, this makes it rather eccentric.

opposite Flags, gas lamps, china and 18th-century chairs surround the fireplace of the American Room.

right The splendid 1750 mahogany desk and bookcase is attractively framed by the Pennsylvanian print curtains.

right bottom A stars-and-stripes cushion, made by the daughter of the current squire, adds an element of fun to the American Room. Rather aptly, her name is Liberty.

opposite This section of the ground-floor passageway has retained its original function as a corridor. The Picture Gallery can be seen in the distance.

Part of Thomas Hardy's *The Woodlanders* is set in Great Hintock, Hardy's name for the beautiful Dorset village of Minterne Magna. A number of scenes take place at the manor, but it would be a mistake to reach for the novel and start thumbing through for references, as the original Minterne House was demolished 20 years after the book was published. The current building, by Arts and Crafts architect Leonard Stokes, was completed for the 10th Lord Digby in 1904.

As a trained architect, Hardy would have found the new house intriguing. At first glance, the entrance facade appears to be Elizabethan, but 17th-century pedimented gables, Georgian-style rustication, Regency-style crenellations and Arts and Crafts windows triumphantly announce that this was a very individual approach to building a manor house at the beginning of a new century.

Leonard Stokes created the structure around a long passageway on each floor, stretching the breadth of the house. Radiating from this central passage are

MINTERNE HOUSE

rooms at the front and back of the house, plus ingenious underfloor heating and plumbing systems. A charming insight into the architect's approach to his commission was revealed when his daughter met the daughter of the current Lord Digby, and asked whether the family had found 'the duct'. Indeed they had. Lord Digby senior loathed bathrooms, and had allowed only two to be installed in his new house. However, Stokes, foreseeing that future generations may not share the same view, had made sure that the infrastructure was in place for further plumbing at a later date.

The current family have always maintained that the house should look lived in, with Lord Digby even going so far as to say that there should be gumboots by the door, preferably children's. A section of the original ground-floor passageway, forming a corridor as originally intended, boasts a charming array of furniture, family photographs and assorted books. On the wall hangs one of the vast marine

oils in the house that proudly commemorate the Digby contribution to the Battle of Trafalgar. Admiral Sir Henry Digby commanded HMS Africa. Here the painting is of a storm after the victory – a timely reminder of humility in the face of nature.

Born in the early 1920s, the current Lord Digby vividly recalls life in the house in its early 20th-century splendour, with its full complement of servants and country-house ritual. Taking the reins after the house had done its bit for the war effort, he made a series of key alterations that remain to this day, including increasing the number of bathrooms! In 1959 he took the shrewd and unsentimental step of blocking off a third of the house and converting it into flats. Stokes' linear approach to the house meant that this was a relatively straightforward procedure, with no unsightly consequences to the exterior, and a rearrangement rather than a rebuilding of the interior. Financially, it secured the future of the house.

One section of the ground-floor passageway was adapted to create a Picture Gallery, housing family portraits and photographs. A framed family tree makes fascinating reading (the families of both Winston Churchill and Diana Spencer were descended from one George Digby, Earl of Bristol), as do various documents pertaining to the Domesday Book. With doors added at one end and a false wall at the other, this area now feels completely separate.

Intriguingly, the end section of the passageway now forms the kitchen of the first of the flats. Light and airy, the kitchen incorporates the large, Gothic-style window that originally lit the whole passageway.

The first of the main rooms leading off the passageway is the Great Hall, continuing the exterior's eccentric mix of styles with vast Gothic windows and Classical arcading. Despite its name and size, it is a cosy affair. Antique carpets and comfortable sofas are surrounded by the soft glow of apricot-coloured walls. The paint colour dates from the 1950s. Lord Digby readily acknowledges that his initial fears of the ceiling looking like 'some kind of ghastly wedding cake' were unfounded. Everywhere there are touching indications of family life. For example, the 40th wedding anniversary of the current Lord and Lady Digby was clearly being celebrated by the attractive iron plaque (showing the family crest of an ostrich with a horseshoe in its beak) propped up in the fireplace.

The original Minterne House was acquired by John Churchill in the early 1600s. Royalists in the Civil War, the Churchills' fortunes revived on the restoration of Charles II. In 1768 the house was bought by Admiral Robert Digby, a younger son of the 7th Baron Digby of Sherborne Castle. In his diary, Robert wrote: 'Visited my new estate, valley very bare, trees not thriving.' Aware of Capability Brown's innovative landscaping at Sherborne Castle, he set about creating his own version. Leonard Stokes' eccentric historicism enabled the 1904 house to sit perfectly well

above left Minterne's Edwardian Arts and Crafts oak panelling and Gothic windows are intriguingly set off by a carved wooden gong from Burma.

above right A commemorative plaque in the fireplace bears the initials of Lord and Lady Digby under the family crest of an ostrich with a horseshoe in its beak.

opposite View of the Great Hall. The painting above the fireplace, a companion to the storm view in the adjoining corridor, depicts the view from Admiral Digby's ship during the Battle of Trafalgar.

right Now lavatories with a musical theme, this room was once the housekeeper's pantry.

below The rich wooden panelling and gilt decoration of the Otis lift is evocative of the sumptuous early 20th-century interiors of London department stores.

opposite, above The hall table is a glorious mix of everyday and treasured objects.

opposite, left The panelling of the staircase gives way once more to the apricot of the Great Hall.

opposite, right The infamous gong 'with devils', brought to Dorset from Burma.

within this 18th-century landscaping. The facades facing the gardens are more Tudor in style than overtly Arts and Crafts. In addition, Stokes echoed features of the old house, such as the large bay window that fronted the original house's tapestry room.

Today, there are constant reminders that this is a family home. On the table at the bottom of the stairs, items such as hats, keys, a torch and another ostrich – plastic this time – share the same space as family regalia in a glass case, recently worn in the Trafalgar bicentenary celebrations. Moving up the stairs, a 1980s artwork is made startling by its (deliberate) juxtaposition alongside a Churchill tapestry. Further family impishness is revealed at the next level – quite literally. The current Lord Digby's grandfather asked a relative travelling in Burma to bring him back a gong, the response to which was a telegram asking whether he wanted 'devils too'. Clearly he could not resist such an interesting proposition.

What is continuously fascinating about a historical house is how the use of spaces changes with the times. At Minterne such changes have a particular charm of their own. The former still (housekeeper's pantry), where Lord Digby remembers jams and pickles being prepared, has recently been converted into a ladies' lavatory. Music is a great love of the current Lady Digby, who organises concerts at Minterne and other venues. Aimed chiefly at concert visitors, the space has been decorated with plates, books and busts commemorating famous composers.

Close by, a wonderful reminder of times past is the splendid Otis lift. After

inventing the safety brake, Elisha Graves Otis sold his first 'safe elevators' in 1853, and in 1884 established sales offices in London and Paris. Early clients included the Eiffel Tower, London Underground and Balmoral Castle. The lift at Minterne is resplendent in gold and mahogany. The gates are heavy and the outside door needs a hard tug to open it, but at the time of its installation it was part of a house that was remarkable for its concealment of modern innovation under a flourish of historical features.

There is far more to Minterne than this brief survey allows, but the Drawing Room is a charming room with which to finish. From a 1960s portrait of the current Lord Digby, to wedding photos of his daughter, this room is about family. Every surface is covered with photographs and books, and the large bay window overlooks the splendid gardens.

Designed after the ideals of William Morris had affected many buildings across the land, the architecture of this Edwardian country house revels in its medley of historical styles as something more artisan than the nationalistic historicism of many Victorian dwellings. A fascinating building, it has been extremely fortunate to have spent so many years in practical and careful hands. At the time of writing, the management of the house is about to pass to the next generation – long may Minterne House last in all its eccentric glory.

MINTERNE HOUSE

opposite, left View of the Drawing Room, a genuinely lived-in space that is much cherished by the owners.

above Facing the gardens, the large bay window frames a table of books and a bronze head dated 1999.

opposite, right A 1970s portrait of Lord Digby, hanging in the Drawing Room, concentrates on his important role of caring for the famous gardens at Minterne.

CONTEMPORARY
PASSIONS

It is a curious thing, but all the buildings in this section predate the 21st century. Their contemporaneity is in the interiors. 43 South Molton Street keeps its address as its name, branding itself immediately as a Central London, Bond Street-area venue, and yet does not style its interior in line with the chic minimalism of its near neighbours. Instead, it takes the English country house as its starting point for a deliberate eccentricity, adding to shabby armchairs and random wall coverings a playful twist of the slightly surreal. In Manchester, the Great John Street Hotel also sets out with an intentional agenda of eccentricity – not for nothing do its owners refer to their three hotels as 'the eclectic hotel collection'. English eccentricity is styled here as something very tactile, coupled with a sensibility towards design from other cultures. Furnishings are of rich velvets and brocades, while fixtures and fittings reflect Moroccan, African and Indonesian influences. Underlying all of this is the historical backdrop of a Victorian schoolhouse, an integral part of the final design concept. Old school photographs and carefully sourced tiling add to the mix, while original features of the building are left exposed.

This theme – of altering the original function, but retaining elements of that function as part of the new design – is shared by several of the featured buildings. The Old Railway Station in West Sussex is a perfect example of creating the unusual out of the historical, restoring it, but giving it new meaning, whilst harking back to its original purpose. Bringing together and restoring a dilapidated station building and three even more dilapidated Pullman carriages to create a charming

CONTEMPORARY

slice of English eccentricity with one's afternoon tea was a huge job, but has proved very successful. Original features such as ticket windows in the former ticket hall and a kitchen hatch in one of the Pullmans do not intrude on the newly designed interiors, but instead add a whimsical or quirky dimension that enriches the experience. Courthouse Hotel Kempinski, in Central London, is another candidate for this definition of eccentricity, where history and new design combine to create something quite unique. The most obvious example of this is the English oak panelling of courtroom number 1 that is now the stylish – yet undeniably eccentric – setting for the hotel's Silk restaurant. And where else would you choose to spend the night in a prison cell, and be happy to pay for the privilege? While the rebirth of these buildings is, of course, a good thing, it is the style and charisma with which they return that is important here.

Though it may have been considered by some as eccentric the first time around, The Deco/Northampton Jesus Centre is certainly an intriguing space now. This example is less about the style with which the building was regenerated – although it goes without saying that this is indeed impressive – and more about the unusual situation of its new function. A recognisable interior style, the Art Deco of 1930s cinemas, is the foundation upon which two very different aspects of life in the 21st century coexist.

above Warm golden drapes and curtains in the Trophy Room at 43 South Molton Street lead to stranger sensations when you notice that the table legs do not quite reach the floor and that a stuffed toy holds up the lamp.

Meanwhile, in a picturesque Cotswold village, behind the facade of the Three Ways House Hotel (its very name quaintly historical) lie the Pudding Club rooms. Ostensibly, this is the result of a nostalgic desire to keep alive a small part of English tradition. However, if the rooms are anything to go by, it is more about the simple pleasures of life. This is an English eccentricity that is playful and not intellectually demanding. Its quirkiness lies in a zany ability to charm.

Finally, the two private homes in this section both reflect the work and lifestyles of their respective owners. Richard Adams, the flamboyant interior designer, is no more going to surround himself with a minimalist cream interior than Julie Arkell, an artist who works in papier-mâché and found objects, would move into a newly built house with a fitted kitchen. The interiors of their homes are fabulous demonstrations of the fact that contemporary living can be individual, different and fun.

PASSIONS

name
43 South Molton Street

address
43 South Molton Street, London W1K 5RS

telephone
020 7647 4343

website
www.43southmolton.com

opening times
Restaurant: midday till late. Members' bar: 6pm till late

description
Members' bar in central London

original structure
1913 terraced house

interior
Russell Sage, 2005

design style
Eccentric country house meets hardware store

Variously known as '43', '43 South Molton' and the full '43 South Molton Street', this riot of colour and cheekiness comprises four floors of eccentricity, right in the centre of London. The eccentric manor-house style of the design is relatively easy to imagine – but hardware store? The answer lies in the restaurant (Bistro & Store), with its 'tapas menu of modern European cuisine'. Here, the shelves surrounding diners are lined with such English favourites as Marmite, Weetabix and Scotts Porridge Oats, jumbled together with hardware-store clutter – all for sale, if you care to round off your meal with a pot of jam or a set of screwdrivers. The entrance to the restaurant is red, rich and reminiscent of a teenager's bedroom, with magazine cut-outs pasted to the wall sporting headlines such as 'the spirit of England', plus a healthy smattering of cut-out 43s, just to remind you where you are, lest you become too caught up in the madness of it all.

The Bistro & Store also showcases young fashion talent on a monthly basis, a not unduly surprising element of the whole 43 South Molton Street experience when one considers its designer. Russell Sage's career has been a glorious mix of fashion, design and eccentric gestures, such as quitting fashion college in his

above The dining tables and chairs of the restaurant are overshadowed by the cluttered shelves and cases.

opposite Vintage clothing, battered furniture, toys and an explosion of colour on the walls greet the diner on arrival.

43 SOUTH MOLTON STREET

youth to join a circus. A one-time antiques dealer, his fashion collections have hit the headlines since his graduation from London's Central Saint Martins in 2000. Themes have included 'hunting and the hunted' and 'making history', with vintage fabrics worked alongside the contemporary. Now described as a celebrated interior and fashion designer, his signature style of English country house chic is stunningly exemplified at 43 South Molton Street.

Upstairs are the members' rooms – the Lounge, the Bar, the intriguingly

named Trophy Room and a small Private Dining Room. By day, the broad window floods the Lounge with natural light, somewhat unexpectedly in a design that relies on colour and clutter and the inevitable association with dimly lit Victorian parlours. But with candles lit and lamps dimmed, this space exudes playfulness. Eccentricity abounds, with 'floating' tables (their legs are raised just an inch or so off the floor by a newly fitted central shaft and foot), a tapestry of a hunting scene made kitsch by hanging it on lush red fabric, and swathes of patterned fabrics

opposite This cosy corner of the private members' Lounge enjoys a quirky country-house style.

below The hunting scene of the tapestry introduces the theme of country-house pursuits, taken up again in the Trophy Room upstairs.

43 SOUTH MOLTON STREET

above Opposite the window hang a bemused Edwardian couple in 'chav' Burberry.

left Glowing in the Bar window are country-park scenes, painted in orange.

above Feint flecks of colour surround the taped postcard that signposts the gentlemen's lavatory.

draped in a seemingly unrelated fashion beside neighbouring blocks of painted colour. Amphora-style vases adorn the purple windowsill alongside piles of old books, while brass trays make precarious tabletops amidst leather pouffes and battered old armchairs.

Across the hallway is the Bar, which elaborates on the country-house theme with a sketchily painted mural on the window panes. In glowing orange paint, it suggests country house and deer park, complete with trees, stream and Palladian bridge. This Bar is intimate and warm, maintaining the playfulness of the Lounge with brightly coloured light bulbs in elaborate brass light fittings, patterned fabrics on the wall, random ceramics such as a brightly painted samovar, and – perhaps the most obvious talking point – the 'chav' painting nailed to the wall. The original Edwardian couple of the portrait have been cheekily redressed in Burberry, making their facial expressions all the more inscrutable.

The Trophy Room, directly above the Lounge, is a secluded space for relaxing or for informal business meetings, accompanied by afternoon tea or cocktails. It is so-named because of the row of disembodied antlers adorning a wall clad in yellow fabric. As a glorious throwback to the eccentricity of another age, they evoke the rather bizarre Victorian antler furniture that can these days be found, for example, in London's V&A Museum. And, of course, they also suggest themes of hunting and conquest. While hunting expeditions demonstrated the wealth

and leisure of the Victorian upper classes, the use of animal parts in furniture, jewellery and costume was also part of their desire for novelty. This theme is picked up again on the landing, where the central feature is a glass monstrance containing exotic stuffed birds amidst lavish foliage.

The playful black-and-white postcard signage of the lavatories gives the first clue of what is to come in the Private Dining Room. A darkly painted affair with a long oak table, it provides seating for 14. While one side of the room is opened up by an engaging use of mirrors, the opposite wall is brought right into the room with a large blown-up photograph of a 1950s gathering of jolly men and women behind tables laden with produce for sale. (Packaging historians would have a field day picking out the tins of Birds Eye custard amongst the trays of eggs, while fashion historians would revel in the hats and printed cottons.) Continuing the theme of black-and-white photography, a playful display of old architectural postcards forms a 3-D design on a smaller wall.

The final room at 43 South Molton Street is for those wishing to enjoy a larger space – the grandly named Ballroom that covers the entire basement level. Dark wood tables and leather banquettes snake their way across the rakishly angled space, and pools of light spill out from translucent light shades housing coloured bulbs. It is definitely play time here, eccentric touches including a lamp fixed to a chair positioned halfway up a wall, and chandeliers hanging at a slant in front of occasional bursts of silver on the walls.

Minutes away from the hustle and bustle of Oxford Street, the calmer and

above left The Private Dining Room has its own DJ booth, and the oak table can be removed to reveal a small dance floor.

above Antlers adorn the wall of the Trophy Room, evoking the leisure pursuits (of all kinds) of the country house.

above The postcard motif, begun on the lavatory doors in the corridor outside, carries through to this display on the dining-room wall

infinitely more elegant South Molton Street is best known for its designer clothes shops. The traditional facade of number 43 does little to indicate the eccentric joys within, where the founders deliberately set out to create a bar that turned convention on its head. The eccentric country-house comforts, convivial atmosphere and joyous explosion of texture and colour combine to make an exceedingly memorable house party.

above Down in the Ballroom, all is funky lighting and snaking angles, ready for partying into the small hours.

name
   Three Ways House Hotel
address
   Mickleton, Chipping Campden,
   Gloucestershire GL55 6SB
telephone
   01386 438429
website
   www.puddingclub.com
sescription
   Country hotel with unusual bedrooms
original structure
   1871 Cotswold house. Hotel since the
   1900s
interior
   Pudding Club themed rooms: Isolde
   Newbury, 1999 onwards
design style
   Classic English puddings become
   hotel decor

Replete with cottages of timber and Cotswold stone, the charming village of Mickleton borders on the Vale of Evesham, famous throughout the last century for its fruit and vegetables. Cauliflowers were once a Mickleton speciality, but things have changed. Where there were cauliflowers, now there are puddings.

The Three Ways House Hotel is the home of the Pudding Club, founded in 1985 to champion the cause of the classic British pudding – jam roly-poly, syrup sponge, sticky toffee pudding, spotted dick – in the face of such evils as frozen strawberry cheesecake and mass-produced Black Forest gateau. It's easy to forget those dark days of English culinary dullness; the success of this delightfully eccentric undertaking is evident from how dated these latter desserts now sound. Membership of the club includes a free pudding, chosen from 'Syrup Sponge', 'Squidgy Chocolate and Nut', or 'Sticky Toffee and Date' (all written references to the puddings use the reverential upper case), while club meetings include a 'modest' three-course meal followed by a ceremonial parade of seven puddings and subsequent tastings. Lashings of custard feature prominently in proceedings. Astonishingly, the Pudding Club has even teamed up with the UK's

above left Moroccan-style furnishings adorn the bed in the Sticky Toffee and Date Room.

opposite Holding up the recipe for the eponymous sticky toffee and date pudding, a colourfully painted Bedouin figure stands next to a sack labelled 'soft brown sugar'.

THREE WAYS HOUSE HOTEL

left top Two monkeys cook up something sticky in the Sticky Toffee and Date Room.

left middle Buttoned up and bewhiskered, Lord Randall looks the very model of Victorian propriety.

left bottom Some might consider it a shame to spoil the surprise lurking behind the bathroom door, but it was an irresistible photograph.

opposite An old battered trunk at the foot of the bed looks ready to be taken at a moment's notice on the next Great Global Adventure.

First Great Western train service, and you can now try the puddings onboard and pick up a Pudding Club Loyalty Card.

The hotel is attractive throughout; however, it is the themed Pudding Rooms that give Three Ways House its very own idiosyncratic charm. Room 10 is the Sticky Toffee and Date Room. A *trompe l'oeil* mural across the ceiling and around the bed seems to alter the contours of the room. The effect of stepping inside a Bedouin tent is extraordinary and appealing, humorous touches such the toy camel on the bed making the experience as fun as it should be. Against the tent backdrop, the recipe for sticky toffee and date pudding is held aloft by a veiled figure. On the other side of the bed, the wall features the recipe for butterscotch sauce.

The paintings continue, with a cheerful camel striding across the bathroom door (his rear end is on the other side), and parrots sitting on high. A wonderful desert scene (that's desert, not dessert) takes up the whole of one wall, dominated by a couple of monkeys heating and tasting the toffee. A light glows in just the right place to represent the sun, while distant palm trees are dotted about in the sand dunes. Details throughout the rest of the room include an Islamic-style central lamp, a ewer on the windowsill, and dark wooden furniture.

Lord Randall's Bedchamber (otherwise known as Room 24) evokes an entirely different world. Designed to create the impression of a Victorian gentleman's bedroom, its most obvious feature is the depiction of the monocled chappy himself, surveying the room from his vantage point on the bathroom door. His copy of *The Times* hints that all is not as formal as it seems: 'Latest for Grand Show: Lord Randall's Bathing Machine'. Step into the bathroom, and something distinctly reminiscent of the saucy seaside postcard is revealed.

The room is named after Lord Randall's pudding, a sponge pudding made

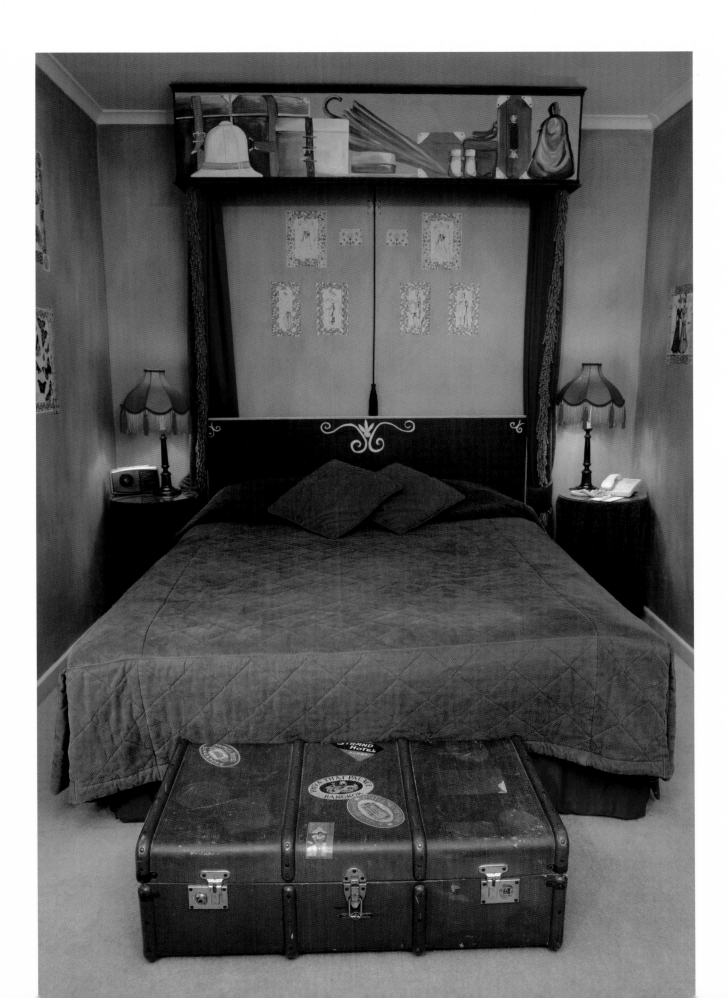

opposite, left Above the bathroom doorway, pots and jars reflect the style of the pelmets in the bedroom.

opposite, right Every Pudding Room incorporates the complete recipe as part of its design.

below In the Spotted Dick and Custard Room, bowls and whisks dance a strange *trompe l'oeil* jig on the pelmets over the bed and window.

opposite, below It is not just the fabrics that convey the spotted aspect of the much-loved spotted dick and custard pudding.

with dried apricots and marmalade. One of the lesser-known classics to be revived by the Pudding Club, its traditional ingredients clearly inspired the hints of traditionalism in this room. Leaf tea in a box labelled 'Ceylon tea' sits on top of a bureau. The furniture is statuesque, and the *trompe l'oeil* depicts the ephemera of a gentleman with the means to travel, including hat boxes, books, a pith helmet and binoculars. The Bedouin lamps of the Sticky Toffee and Date Room have here become fringed lampshades. The walls cleverly suggest the picture collection of this imaginary Victorian gentleman with engravings of natural history, fashionably dressed young women, architectural monuments, Egyptian friezes and so on.

Originally built in 1871, Three Ways House has been a hotel since the early 1900s. No doubt spotted dick and custard (also known as spotted dog) would have been on the menu in those early days. Room 17 is a bright and sunny room with custard-coloured walls and a dotty fabric to suggest the dried fruit of the pudding, but it is the Dalmatians who steal the limelight. In the mural by the bed, they appear to be guarding the pudding that dominates the table. Pudding bowls, spoons and a jug of custard complete the bedroom ensemble.

The bathroom walls are painted with kitchen shelves, from which hang ladles,

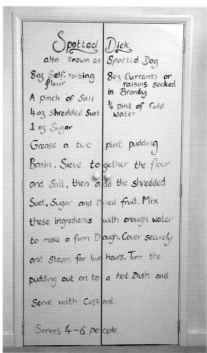

rolling pins, a cook's apron and whisks. Another fun feature is the adjoining closet. On its doors is the recipe for spotted dick, and within there is a surprise. With just enough room for bunk beds, complete with Disney Dalmatian duvet covers, this is a fun space for children. Veering slightly away from puddings – although its theme is a key ingredient in many of the classics – the Chocolate

Suite is the newest of the rooms. The hotel's website wonders if you have ever dreamt of going to sleep in a box of chocolates, though to a chocoholic this is not the most obvious reaction to the box's contents. However, the room is tempting in many other ways. The bed is extraordinary, with a beribboned headboard and 'chocolate' cushions. On the inside of the bedroom door, 'Three Ways' chocolate makes its debut, and in the bathroom, specially commissioned tiles feature the same Three Ways motif. But it is not just the tiles that are extremely chocolaty – the organic shampoo and body wash are chocolate based as well, and smell delicious.

Three Ways House cheerfully promotes a stay in one of the Pudding Rooms as having all the fun and none of the calories, but even the most savoury-toothed person would find it hard not to yield to a scrumptious pudding after such a visual onslaught on the taste buds.

above Perhaps the most mouth-watering feature in the Chocolate Suite are the 'chocolates' on the bed. Designed by a local theatre costumier, these cushions look truly delicious.

below The specially commissioned tiles in the Chocolate Suite bathroom were made by British firm Ceramore, founded in 2002 to resurrect tile-making processes that had been lost to British manufacturing for generations.

opposite The inside of the door has been cleverly adapted to look like the squares of a chocolate bar.

THREE WAYS HOUSE HOTEL

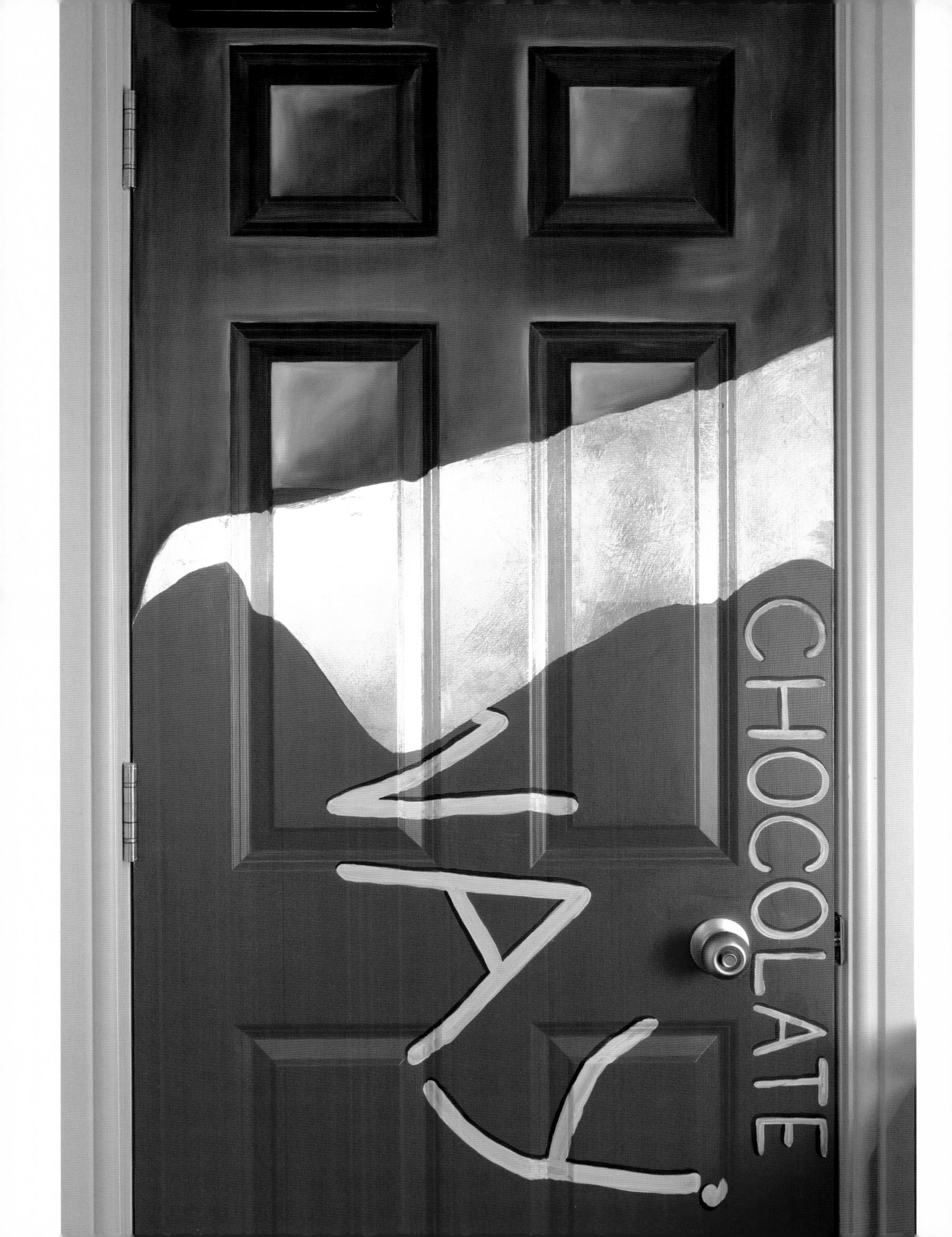
YAY!
CHOCOLATE

name
Old Railway Station

address
Petworth, West Sussex GU28 0JF

telephone
01798 342346

website
www.old-station.co.uk

description
Victorian station and 20th-century Pullman carriages converted into accommodation

original structure
Station building, 1894. Pullmans 1912, 1914 and 1925

interior
Lou Rapley, 1996 onwards

design style
Bed and breakfast on the Orient-Express

From the first experiments in steam locomotion to the launch of Eurostar, the railways have been a source of fascination for generations of travellers across Britain. By the mid-19th century this new feature of the British landscape was a key player in the history of architecture and design. For example, on its completion in 1868 St Pancras railway station, with its massive single-span roof of glass and ironwork, was the largest enclosed structure in the world. Its adjoining hotel was designed by prolific Gothic-revival architect George Gilbert Scott. Meanwhile, carriage interior design had become synonymous with the 'Englishness' of the railways (by this time a major British export), and iconic posters and typefaces graced every station in the country.

The Grade II-listed station building at Petworth was constructed in 1894, during the boom years of the London, Brighton & South Coast Railway company, which pioneered the running of the all-Pullman train in England. A prosperous area of West Sussex, Petworth is perhaps best known for its country estate where JMW Turner spent much of his time in the 1820s and 1830s, as a guest of the 3rd Earl of Egremont, sketching and painting the house and parklands. Unfortunately, the demise of the station was partly due to the insistence of a later Earl that it be built out of earshot of the town – leaving villagers with a 3-kilometre (2-mile) trudge. The last passenger train ran in February 1955, though goods services lingered on for another 11 years. In the 1990s, the building was converted to the Old Railway Station, a stylish bed and breakfast.

Behind the main building, the former platform makes an attractive terrace, overlooking a beautiful sunken lawn where once the railway track passed by. The cutting continues to the left and, together with the former siding, this area has now been put to rather splendid use. In 1998, new track was laid down by London

above Throughout all three restored Pullmans, details from the original decor provide wonderful touches. This window is in Mimosa 1.

opposite Through the bedroom window of Mimosa 1, Flora can be glimpsed across the old platform.

OLD RAILWAY STATION

173

Underground staff in the siding, in readiness for the lowering, by 70-tonne crane, of two genuine Pullman carriages – Alicante (built in 1912) and Mimosa (1914). Brought by truck from Cornwall, where they had remained abandoned for many years and fallen prey to squatters and vandals, the carriages underwent a seven-month restoration to convert them to stunning bedroom suites. In 2002, a third Pullman, Flora (1925), was lowered into the parallel stretch of railway cutting to complete the ensemble.

Read any description of the Orient-Express and you will read of gleaming Pullman 'cars' with their umber and cream livery and interiors typified by plush upholstery, intricate marquetry, solid brass fittings and soft-shaded lamps. Both the Orient-Express and the Bluebell Railway assisted in the restoration of the Pullmans at the Old Railway Station, the individual characters of which have been created through tasteful historical suggestion. Mimosa (divided into two suites) has a Regency feel, its soft-blue walls and prints inspired by the discovery of Herculaneum. White detailing sets off ornately carved mirrors and Regency-style furnishings, accentuating the curved carriage ceiling and adding highlights to the woodwork. Alicante is more Georgian in style, with a painted gold-and-cream interior and mahogany furniture.

Onboard Flora, the bedroom has the rich marquetry that we associate with the Orient-Express, and is accessorised with battered suitcases, Victorian prints,

top Original fixtures and fittings were polished and restored as part of the conversion into accommodation, simultaneously playing a useful and nostalgic role.

above Positioned in the corridor that leads to the main carriage/bedroom, the old kitchen galley hatch onboard Mimosa is now a fun feature of the bathroom.

right The elegantly appointed bathroom onboard Flora utilises the Pullman colour scheme.

opposite, top Flora is the most valuable Pullman. With the original marquetry walls still intact, this Pullman really does evoke luxury travel on the Orient-Express.

opposite, bottom Flora was named after the exquisite motifs of small flowers that surround the mirrors and windows and adorn the rich inlaid panels.

gilt mirrors and ornate glass lampshades. The old sliding windows are visible through the Venetian blinds, and other original fittings include the luggage rack in the small lobby by the entrance door, a space that cleverly houses a narrow mahogany wardrobe and chest of drawers.

Between the lobby and the main carriage/bedroom is the bathroom, positioned where a small compartment would have been. Again, the unmistakable Pullman windows can be seen (for this room the glass is now frosted), along with the familiar curved ceiling and sections of marquetry. It is an engaging conversion of a small space.

Onboard Mimosa, the area between the lobby and the main carriage used to be a small galley kitchen. Here, the bathroom now rather charmingly retains the original kitchen hatch.

opposite The spiral staircase snakes past densely packed bookshelves to the ground floor of the old station.

above left At the base of the stairwell, set against exposed brickwork and wooden flooring, are suitcases, games and books, and an old porter's trolley.

above right Built on top of the original Victorian station building, and accessed by the spiral staircase, is the attractively beamed Upper Room with its large mirror and angled skylights.

right below Leading out to the terrace (originally the station platform), the wooden door displays an old Petworth station sign.

It took five years to restore the station building. Bedrooms occupy the site of the gentlemen's urinals plus a new floor built above this area. Lit from above by recessed skylights with attractive lace edging, the striking beam design of the Upper Room complements the vertical wooden cladding of the original building. Access to this room is via a book-lined spiral staircase, its base in the area that used to be the ladies' waiting room. The station sign can be seen on the door that once led to the platform. Fascinating framed documents about the history of the station hang above the old brick fireplace, while suitcases, books, puzzles and games surround an old porter's trolley.

The former waiting room and ticket hall has a 6-metre (20-foot) vaulted ceiling and original, beautiful wooden flooring. At one end it is now a spacious sitting-room area, with sofas and newspapers gathered around the fireplace. At the other end it is the breakfast room, set with assorted pine tables and chairs. The whole room is bright and light, with pale-pink walls and large windows on either side. With the old ticket windows still in situ, the dining area backs on to the former stationmaster's office that now forms the kitchen.

The style is Victorian colonial, with decorative dried flowers in a huge black

above Now in a striking pink, the tongue-and-groove walls of the former ticket office and waiting room have been transformed to create a cheerful breakfast room and lounge.

top left In summer, the shuttered windows that line opposite sides of the room let in a wonderful amount of light, while on a winter's night the large vaulted room is made cosy by the old brass lamps and a crackling fire.

top right Old-style entertainment as well as fittings and fixtures add to the character of this thoroughly engaging bed and breakfast.

right Picked out in white, the former ticket windows are an attractive feature of the breakfast room.

urn, candlesticks, binoculars, old photographs of the station, brass lamp-bases, a model of a Pullman carriage, books on trains and countless other bits and pieces (some of which were brought back from travels overseas). A particularly spectacular feature are the brass light fittings. These came from a Plymouth salvage yard, and had formerly been used as the external lighting for a station building. Spaced at regular intervals between the shuttered windows, they bring real character to the space. Engraved portraits and an old gramophone help to turn a once functional space into one of warmth and geniality.

name
Courthouse Hotel Kempinski
address
19–21 Great Marlborough Street, Soho,
London W1F 7HL
telephone
020 7297 555
website
www.courthouse-hotel.com
description
Courthouse and other buildings
converted to a five-star hotel
original structure
Courthouse, 1912–13
interior
Sunita Sanger and Ward Design
Services, 2005
design style
Eccentric conversion with a dash of
black humour

opposite The Lobby includes blue decorative
glassware, rakishly stacked suitcases, chairs of
an attractive and extremely comfortable shell
design, a striking glass whirlpool-pattern
screen and limestone flooring.

above Elements of nature also
appear in the lounge, with its
stone pillars and water features in
pots set into the wall.

Open a brand-new five-star hotel minutes away from Bond Street, Regent Street
and Carnaby Street, and there should be a decent amount of publicity. Locate the
hotel in the former Great Marlborough Street Magistrates' Court – in which a
whole host of headline-grabbing court cases took place – and things should
really heat up. And add a little dash of eccentricity while converting courtrooms
and prison cells into a luxury hotel, and you get the blaze of publicity that
surrounded the opening of the Courthouse Hotel Kempinski in 2005.

Today's stylish visitors are not the first fashionistas to have swept through the
imposing double doors of the courthouse. In 1895, that most famous of late
Victorian dandies, Oscar Wilde, instigated his disastrous criminal libel charge
against the Marquess of Queensbury here. And 60 years earlier, a frequent visitor
to the courtrooms was William Nelson, a member of a group of prosperous
London thieves dubbed 'the Swell mob', who dressed stylishly, lived in the best

COURTHOUSE HOTEL KEMPINSKI

parts of town and cruised the streets of London with girls on their arms. In contemporary records of social reformers trying to understand the workings of the criminal mind, much is made of Nelson's fashionable dress sense and good manners. In 1969, creating perhaps some of the most iconic images of the late 1960s, Marianne Faithful and Mick Jagger were snapped by the world's paparazzi as they descended the steps of the courthouse after Jagger was fined £200 for drugs offences.

In April 2000, this historic court ceased to exist, but the building did not stay empty for long. Bought by London-based Surejogi Hotels (run by the Sanger family), it became the second Surejogi hotel to partner up with luxury hotel group Kempinski Hotels. While the Kempinski classic, contemporary design is evident in the bedrooms and suites, there is an altogether more adventurous, individual approach to the ground-floor spaces. The original courthouse entrance hall now leads into the lobby on the right, and Carnaby's, one of the hotel's three restaurants, to the left. Both are light, bright spaces, illuminated by the huge windows of the facade. Chocolate-brown and cream colours make the low-ceilinged lounge one of elegant relaxation and comfort.

COURTHOUSE HOTEL KEMPINSKI

top The private booths were formerly women's holding cells.

above Each cell door comes complete with grill and spy hole.

opposite, top View from inside the prison gates of the bar, looking back into the lounge.

opposite, bottom An elongated glass bar (run by an all-women team) stretches along the back wall.

But all is not quite as tranquil as it seems. At the far end of the lounge lurks the bar, its stone facing and original prison gates generating a very different presence. Its interior is mainly marble walls, black Indian mica slate flooring and black-and-white low leather seating. Amongst the cocktails is 'Behind Bars', a fusion of Xanté (pear cognac) with crème de cacao and bars of grated nutmeg. Together with the prison bars at the entrance, this is a distinct hint that there is more to this watering hole than chic, contemporary styling.

Along the right-hand wall, three private booths are, in fact, the last three remaining prison cells in the building. Think of the narrow confines of an Alcatraz cell, then swap the bed for smart leather cushioned seating, fill the lavatory with shiny pebbles, and place an ice bucket on top. In a wonderful twist, the cells can be hired for complete privacy; in the past, money may have set the ladies in these women-only holding cells free. Soundproof and highly original, the booths are a fabulously quirky use of the building's original features.

During the conversion from courthouse to five-star hotel, there must have been a brainstorming of words associated with the law. 'Lobby' and 'bar' were a gift; 'Silk', as the name for the smartest of the restaurants, was inspired. In British law, 'taking silk' means the promotion of a barrister with 10 or more years of experience to the level of QC (Queen's Counsel). Traditionally, a QC wears a silk gown, whereas a junior barrister wears a cotton gown.

Silk is located within the infamous Number One Courtroom. Christine Keeler appeared here in 1963 over sex allegations that led to the Profumo scandal becoming public. Nine years later the case against John Lennon for exhibiting sexually explicit pictures in the London Art Gallery was dismissed in this room. Converting such a distinctive space into a restaurant was an unusual challenge, made all the more so by the building's Grade II listed status, which meant that many features had to be retained as part of English Heritage regulations. The result is a unique and spectacular room, made instantly appealing by its huge vaulted glass ceiling, original English oak panelling – and judge's bench, dock and witness stand. (The latter is now set as a table for one.)

The judge's bench provides a discrete space for out-of-sight cooler cabinets, plus the storage of menus and other dining ephemera. The restaurant staff now enter and exit through doors that once admitted bewigged and robed officials, and are equally resplendent in yellow silk jackets with mandarin collars. A golden Buddha presides over the proceedings, making apparent a further play on words. The restaurant has as its theme the Silk Route, its menu inspired by this historic trade network between East and West to produce an eclectic mix of Italian,

COURTHOUSE HOTEL KEMPINSKI

above left Today the Waiting Room is an elegant atrium used for breakfast and afternoon tea.

above right The auditorium of Release, Courthouse Hotel Kempinski's 100-seater private cinema.

opposite, top View of Silk, the former Number One Courtroom.

opposite, bottom Gilt lettering, designating such court officialdom as 'Counsel and Solicitors', remains on the courtroom woodwork and now surrounds the dining tables.

Middle Eastern and Asian cuisine. The handcrafted map of the Silk Route above the judge's bench was specially commissioned for the restaurant, and expertly brings the culinary theme into the legal setting.

Next door to Silk is the Waiting Room, which serves breakfast and afternoon tea. Palm trees in the centre of the room shade the terrazzo floor from the natural light streaming through another vaulted glass ceiling. In its previous life, the room would have been a far less relaxing place, as defendants and witnesses nervously waited to appear before the judge.

The conversion to Courthouse Hotel Kempinski has made the property nearly three times larger than the original building. The uppermost storey is the elegant roof terrace, and underground are the conference rooms, known as 'the Chambers'. Twelve of the thirteen suites are located in the former judges' robing rooms. The grandest suite, the Lalique Penthouse Suite, is sited within the former London residence of the Metropolitan Police Commissioner. As its name suggests, this suite boasts crystal chandeliers, furnishings, lights and doorknobs by Lalique. Original Robert Adam fireplaces adorn several of the other suites. Built on a site that once combined a police station, holding cells and a shooting range, a brand new wing houses the 103 bedrooms.

The last of the stylish and quirky suite of ground-floor rooms is Release, a wittily named private cinema. With its aubergine carpeting, suede walls and apple-green leather seating, this space is used for screenings, product launches and corporate presentations, and also hosts a regular cinema club showing cult films from around the world. Somehow it seems entirely fitting to have a private cinema in an environment that embraces its distinctive heritage with such style and a sense of fun.

The two entrances to this building open up two entirely different worlds and, in parts of the building, these parallel worlds even occupy the same space, although not at the same time.

The main facade and foyer of this magnificently restored 1930s cinema, looking every bit as Art Deco as you would expect, is the entrance to the Northampton Jesus Centre. Today's owners of the building, the Jesus Fellowship Church (or the Jesus Army), are known for their work in areas such as homelessness and drug abuse. Intriguingly, they saw the potential of this Grade II-listed building as a place to restore both the soul and the architectural gem that began life as the Savoy Cinema. To the right of the main facade the other entrance, with automatic doors and modern box-office decor, announces the fully integrated conference centre, theatre and multipurpose venue that is The Deco. Billed as 'high-tech with heritage', The Deco is a stunning venue for corporate, social and theatrical events, and is run by an independently owned facilities-management company.

Back in May 1936, things were rather simpler. Heralded as 'Northampton's only super cinema', the Savoy opened to the delight of the local press. Designed by William Riddell Glen, the house architect of Associated British Cinemas (ABC), it came complete with a Compton organ that rose with a fanfare of music and lights from the pit. On the stage, three pairs of tabs (curtains) were available – massive house tabs filling the proscenium arch, screen tabs behind for cinema use, and a third pair for live performances. Check out the venue list of the Beatles 1963 UK Autumn Tour, and you'll see that it includes the Northampton ABC (the name changed in the 1950s). The *Northampton Chronicle & Echo* recorded that the concert culminated with 'Twist and Shout', during '26 minutes of mass frenzy'.

name
The Deco/Northampton Jesus Centre

address
Abington Square, Northampton NN1 4AE

telephone
01604 622 749

website
www.thedeco.co.uk/
www.jesuscentre.org.uk

opening times
All year round (also available for hire)

description
Restored Art Deco cinema, now a dual-purpose venue

original structure
The Savoy Cinema, 1936

interior
Refurbishment and conservation by GSS Architects (in consultation with English Heritage), 2004

design style
Classic Art Deco cinema with new (split) personality

opposite and above The auditorium is a flexible space, where the stalls seating can easily be replaced by tables and chairs for parties.

THE DECO/ NORTHAMPTON JESUS CENTRE

187

Sadly, as with so many cinemas across Britain, the Savoy's days were numbered, and in 1995, after screening *Pulp Fiction*, *Terminal Velocity* and *Just Cause*, it closed down. It did not take long for the disused building to become derelict. In the auditorium, part of the fibrous plaster collapsed under a leaking section of the roof, pigeons nested, and a vixen and her cub also took up residence here. Having witnessed 60 years of movie history, not to mention Beatlemania, the auditorium has been restored to its former glory and is now the epicentre of the building. A 900-seat venue, it is a spectacular setting for wedding parties, concerts and theatre shows, as well as worship.

Although the cinema was converted to a three-screen complex in 1974, much of the original stage area was thankfully left untouched due to the persistence of the manager, one Ken Porter, who was an active member of amateur operatic societies. Along with photographic records and Glen's original plans, the surviving elements of the building were a major factor in the planning of the recent £4 million refurbishment and conservation programme. Traditional materials and construction methods were used, old paint was stripped to restore the venue to its 1930s colour scheme, and much of the existing plasterwork was saved.

The auditorium is now fully equipped with state-of-the-art sound, lighting and projection systems. To blend in with the decor, the speaker boxes are a delicate shade of blush pink and, on the stage, black and grey neutral drapes are set off by a pair of old gold-velour house tabs. The orchestra pit, covered to form a forestage, can still be used, and the original organ lift is still in place, though another lift above it now brings a baptismal tank to stage level. But perhaps the most immediately noticeable feature of the auditorium is the Art Deco styling of the massive ante-proscenium, with its two very striking arched lighting coves. In

above Despite years of neglect and resulting damage, a surprising number of the skyscraper-motif ports in the building's original doors have survived.

opposite Viewed from the highest balcony, the auditorium's Art Deco components come together to form a stunning ensemble.

below left The red and gilt tip-down seats, with their Art Deco designs, are a wonderful reminder of the building's heyday as the Savoy Cinema.

below right The Art Deco lighting coving is one of the most striking features of the auditorium, and was much photographed (in black-and-white) in its early days.

THE DECO / NORTHAMPTON JESUS CENTRE

the cinema's heyday, these were lit by ever-changing colours, especially during intervals and organ interludes.

During the restoration, boarded-up areas revealed hidden features such as the grand staircase side balconies. Many of the art deco skyscraper port motifs in the doors had survived. A new balcony was added to the circle, to house the stylish renovated seating as well as the sound-control and lighting decks.

Today, the doors at the back of the auditorium lead to distinctly separate parts of the building. On the ground floor, the doors access the rear stalls area that was converted to two small cinemas in the 1970s. This space now forms two suites as part of The Deco's conference facilities. The original Art Deco trough cove lighting on the ceiling remains, but is split in two by the 1970s dividing wall. It is through the doors at this level that visitors to The Deco enter the auditorium. A floor above, the doors are those of the Jesus Centre's Circle Café, forming the centre's main access to the auditorium. The uppermost floor comprises training rooms and offices for the Jesus Centre.

Earlier cinema-goers would have entered the auditorium via the stalls or circle doors, having first passed through the striking entrance foyer. However, where posters and photographs of movie stars once adorned the walls, posters and notices of a rather different nature now greet visitors, as today this area is the entrance foyer for the Jesus Centre. The high arched ceiling and original 1930s decorative balconies are a clear visual indication of how the foyer once looked, and vast pot plants resemble those in photographs of the original. Either side of the central stairs, the former pay boxes for the stalls and circle are now cupboards. The ascent to the level above, magnificent with

above At the top of the entrance foyer stairs, the original ironwork and balcony signage stylishly lead the visitor to the circle foyer.

opposite, top left Today the circle foyer is the Circle Café. Complete with the familiar skyscraper-motif ports, the original doors lead into the auditorium.

opposite, far right The double-height entrance foyer was a signature design of ABC's house architect WR Glen.

opposite, near left Including an area devoted to community art exhibitions, the Circle Café makes imaginative use of the circle foyer space.

its original signage and 1930s ironwork, leads to the circle foyer, now the Jesus Centre's Circle Café.

When the cinema first opened, each day, at 1.45pm, the staff of 25 was paraded in the circle foyer by the manager. Old photographs of this area show a wildly patterned carpet and wicker furniture flush against the walls, and the 2004 building work uncovered the original 'Circle' sign and vomitory doors also visible in the photographs. The sign is now restored and relit, above doors that are exactly as they were (with the exception of the fire regulations signs and metal panels at the base).

This is a building that leads an unusual, yet very successful, double life, despite the fact that planning permission was initially rejected. Presumably its critics have been silenced by the breathtaking restoration of this marvellous example of 20th-century interwar sumptuousness.

name
  Richard Adams' house
address
  Chelsea, London
website
  www.richardadamsinteriors.com
description
  Interior designer's showcase
  apartment
original structure
  Victorian mansion flats
interior
  Richard Adams
design style
  18th and 19th centuries meet the
  1950s and 1960s

Three years ago, the most notable features of this small Chelsea apartment were snails on the living-room carpet, water running down the bedroom wall, and coats of lead-based paint. Enter Richard Adams, an American-born interior designer looking to create a fun new living space for himself that would also serve as a flamboyant venue for his business. The resulting explosion of colour is an eccentric fusion of stylistic references that playfully offers the exact opposite of the traditional minimalist solution to small-space design. But then, everything about this apartment reflects – literally, as many of the walls are mirrored – the larger-than-life personality of its charming and vivacious owner. It is no accident that three books turned around to face into the living room are entitled *Snobs*, *Shocking!* and *Unsuitable Company*.

The living room is resplendent in pea-green silk, and natural light and mirrored reflections sparkle in the rich hues of the floor and ceiling. Included in the mix are dramatic paintings by Bernard Buffet (who said of painting that 'we do not analyse it, we feel it'), hung close to black-and-white photographs of family and friends. A 1950s Venini chandelier is silhouetted against swags of silk at the

above The glass bookcase is a treasure trove of books and ephemera, and gives a stylish finish to the wall.

opposite View of the living room, facing the mirrored wall. The chimney breast comprises a triptych of glass images and the black rectangular opening for the fire. Everything else is a reflection.

RICHARD ADAMS' HOUSE

window, and a modern, black-painted hearth is framed by the mirrored reflection of a gilt-and-black Rococo table. There are little suggestions of fun everywhere – monkey candlesticks, a masquerade mask, a hugely overblown vase of fresh lilies. Entertaining is a key function of the apartment, and just as in the glittering interiors of bygone centuries, candlelight and firelight are integral to the effect.

The apartment is not simply a showpiece, it is a lived-in space – and not only by its creator. Mordred and Merlin, the Persian cats, make an appearance from time to time, one loving the limelight, the other lurking hesitantly in the presence of strangers. It is clear that it is the former trait that typifies their flamboyant master. Raised and educated in New York, Adams worked in fashion, before moving into advertising. This was a period during which he met and got to know some of the great icons of the 20th century: 'from Diana Vreeland to Andy Warhol, Salvador Dalí, Truman Capote and Billy Baldwin. I even worked with some of them. More importantly, I observed, absorbed and never forgot their special brand of chic – something which is proving more and more elusive today.' Adams' unique fusion of 20th-century glamour and earlier historical opulence is completely infectious.

Reflected in the mirrored walls of the living room are tantalising glimpses of red – the bedroom beckons. Entered through simple dividing doors, this fabulously ostentatious room is dominated by the crystal sunburst clock above the bed. While the association with the court of Versailles is obvious, it also brings to mind the star and garter of royal portraits. The window swags are held in place with golden tiebacks worthy of the Sun King himself, and wooden blinds hang over sash windows painted the same deep-red of the bed and walls. Small black columns adorned with lampshade-bearing busts open up to form vital

above left Mirrored red-on-red turns the bedroom into a glorious cocoon.

above middle The 1950s chandelier by Venini. Every twisting section is a separate piece of glass.

above right A picture of opposites: leopard print and silk, mirror and glass, geometry and ruching.

opposite Geometric mid-20th-century design mixes with Rococo ornamentation, while the red background of the Buffet painting picks up the red of the bedroom.

opposite A Baroque altarpiece gleams amidst the white tiles and chrome towel rails.

above left View of the hall. Light catches the mirrored bedroom door, adding to the playful fantasy of white column and Baroque tableau in the bathroom.

above middle The traditional hall mirror becomes a rather more flamboyant affair.

above right A kitchen with a difference.

storage space. Adams throws open both rooms for entertaining, and delightedly explains that he has found a petite housekeeper who fits perfectly in the setting for such occasions.

Guests no doubt love the bathroom. Alongside classic white and chrome – and a clever conversion of a lift shaft to accommodate the lavatory – a Baroque chest of drawers with Chinese inlay stands on a faux cowhide. Not only are these features glorious in their unorthodox surroundings, they also prevent an uninvited minimalism breaking through. A decorative glass lamp-base, Chinese porcelain, framed photographs and scent bottles all provide an eccentric twist to this small space.

Across the hall, with its single white column, rich bronze papering and stunning mirror, is the last of the apartment's rooms. Store cupboards contain files, the work surface is home to computer and other desk accessories, and the oven provides handy storage for anything that needs temporarily clearing away. This is no ordinary kitchen environment. Laudably, it makes an ideal home office – the fridge within arm's length of the keyboard. The kitchen is, in fact, fully equipped, but it is refreshing to see framed back-and-white photographs under the kitchen cupboards instead of a toaster or spice rack, and a bust (that might be Paris), rather than a plastic beaker with a dish mop in it, centred behind the taps! This is eccentricity at its absolute finest.

name
Great John Street Hotel

address
Great John Street, Manchester M3 4FD

telephone
0161 831 3211

website
www.greatjohnstreet.co.uk

description
Original structure laid bare and converted to a luxury hotel

original structure
Victorian schoolhouse

interior
Sally O'Loughlin, 2005

design style
New York meets vintage chic

Late in 2004, former pupils of a Manchester city centre school that had closed in the 1960s would no doubt have been surprised and delighted at being invited to a reunion at their old building. But this was no ordinary reunion. Their memories and stories were to become a part of the design of the new hotel being created within the old school's walls.

The former pupils did indeed provide plenty of ideas and anecdotes to weave in with hotel owner and designer Sally O'Loughlin's design concept. The seeds of her 'New York loft meets vintage chic' idea had been germinating for some time, but finding the right building had proved a challenge. Sally had previously worked for Granada Television, which, after the school closed, had taken over the building, renaming it the Old School House. She remembers the building with low ceilings, canteen, photographic studios and so on. However, to her amazement, up for sale and stripped of its 20th-century layers, the building was a classic Victorian school structure, with high ceilings, exposed brick walls, vast ceiling girders and tall windows. Separate staircases for girls and boys were still in situ, the girls' stairs ending a storey lower than that for the boys, since the latter led up to a boys-only playground on the roof. Former pupils recall that this area could be quite an ice rink on wintery days.

opposite Room 30 is dominated by a French carved bed, while the bathroom area is located up the stairs.

GREAT JOHN STREET HOTEL

opposite, top The old school windows add to the luxurious sense of space.

opposite, bottom Original Victorian wooden floors have been preserved in many of the rooms.

right In Room 30, the view from the twin baths includes a giant wicker and peacock-feather mannequin.

The height of the schoolrooms, the ceiling girders and the solid brickwork lent themselves well to the loft look, while the original fireplaces and large windows provided the ideal backdrop for vintage-style fabrics and furnishings. Designated either Baby Grand, Boudoir Grand or Grand, all of the individually designed rooms are split into two levels joined by a carpeted staircase. Sometimes the bed is on high, and sometimes it is the bathroom that is elevated. For example, in Room 30 the bedroom is on the lower level, below the bathroom area, and has a white-painted bed and wardrobe, deep-red patterned curtains and red desk chair. Up the stairs, the space is dominated by twin baths, with claw feet and back-to-back taps. Mirrored cabinets set against school-style tiling and a separate lavatory and shower complete the ensemble.

The huge, carved French bed, with Egyptian linen and handsprung mattresses, fits comfortably within the space, lit by the old schoolroom windows

below The school-style brickwork of the corridors and staircases is given a much-needed warmth by plush carpeting.

right The colossal 'egg bath' is surrounded by rough wooden blocks for toiletries and towels.

opposite In Room 19, the lower area is a comfortable sitting room, with shower and lavatory tucked out of sight, while upstairs the bed and bath share the same space.

and beautifully set off by the original Victorian floors. Throughout the hotel, striking colours and opulent fabrics bring rich warmth to the natural colours of stone and wood.

The hotel owners' personal experiences of France and Sri Lanka have led to an interest in both colonial and classic French design. Thai tiling, African stone, Moroccan-style lighting and oriental hangings share the same setting as old

black-and-white photographs of the Manchester schoolchildren who once occupied the building. These were the children of itinerant barge people, or 'water gypsies' as they were sometimes known, who worked on the nearby trade barges that once populated the busy Bridgewater Canal. Though Manchester led the way during the Industrial Revolution, the by-product of this boom in trade and commerce was a working class that suffered acute poverty and oppression.

A different layout is introduced in Room 19, where both bed and bath share the upper level. The look here is one of plain fabrics in brown, gold and burgundy, and the dominant feature is the 'egg bath', mounted on an area of wooden flooring on the opposite side of the room to the bed. It took eight men to carry this colossal African stone bath up the stairs. In one of the other rooms, the chimney breast is the focal point for the bath. Below, the mix of fabrics and textures creates an attractive sitting-room area. A screen breaks up the geometry where one wall meets another, and on the hearth of an Art Nouveau fireplace sits a sculpture of a woman's torso.

In keeping with the school theme, the hotel's three meeting rooms are the Girls' Classroom, the Boys' Classroom and – largest of all, naturally – the Headmaster's Office. One of the walls in each of the rooms is a *trompe l'oeil* bookcase effect, and furnishings include black leather chairs. Meanwhile, in the lounge, a genuine bookcase is complete with stepladder, assorted books and a display of sports trophies, such as would be found in a bookcase in a school hall or corridor. The Art Nouveau fireplace features again here, while the fabrics and furnishings continue the styling of the bedrooms.

top left The brown, burgundy and gold of Room 19 is set off by chrome fittings such as a small side table.

opposite, top right The sunlight streams in through the old school windows onto the original flooring and the fireplace.

opposite, below In this room, the claw-footed bath is placed across the original chimney breast, and wooden window slats add to the earth colours of the bathroom space.

above The hotel lounge is a riot of colour and textured fabrics, with lamps, candles and small tables.

above left The brickwork and ornate sofa in the front reception area introduce the theme of historic building and contemporary eclectic design.

above right The flamboyant railings run up the stairs and around the balcony that overlooks the bar. On this upper level are further comfortable seating areas, plus the breakfast room.

opposite Mushroom-coloured walls provide a soft backdrop to the rich colours of the champagne and cocktail bar. To the left (out of view) is the semicircular bar.

below Heavy vintage fabrics are a key feature of the building's conversion from school to luxury hotel.

Through the lounge door is a glimpse of the bar, the central focus of the ground floor. Here, the splendid gilt mirrors, black and brown armchairs, a huge candelabra and the gleaming semicircular bar are overlooked by the spectacular decorative ironwork of a mezzanine-level balcony. Like several other high-profile venues in Manchester, the whole building is non-smoking, a forward-looking approach typical in a city that is undergoing huge regeneration.

The former boys-only playground is now a spectacular rooftop terrace, described by the hotel as an 'urban oasis with showcase garden', complete with custom-made water feature, bar and moveable planters. Not only can guests enjoy panoramic views of the city; they also have a bird's-eye view of the on-set filming of that most enduring of English soap operas, 'Coronation Street', as the Granada Television studios are just a stone's throw from the hotel. Available for private al-fresco dining, the rooftop space also has a meeting room that holds 40 people, as well as a hot tub and gym room.

Back on the ground floor, black slate flooring pulls together the decorative scheme of the bar and continues out to the front reception area, an immediately engaging introduction to the building, with its exposed brick walls, fabric wall hangings and luxurious sofa. Nearby are lavatories with their cubicle doors a few inches short of the floor – a playful reference to the old school lavatory doors. Subject of much publicity and already frequented by many celebrities, the old schoolhouse is certainly alive and kicking.

name
Julie Arkell's house
address
Islington, London
description
Artist's private residence stuffed with eclectic and vintage items
original structure
1850s townhouse
interior
Julie Arkell, 1999 onwards
design style
House as art and art as home

It is something of a rarity to encounter an individual living in a London townhouse that has been in the family since 1919. Many inhabitants of London view their life in the capital as a rather shorter-term commitment. Artist Julie Arkell's grandparents moved into the house as tenants, in an area of London that has experienced dramatic changes over the years. Much of the land in Islington was bought by the Clothworkers' Company, which then leased out sections to building firms and other companies. Built in 1850, the house is part of a row of elegant, white terraced housing that has survived demolition, bombs and dry rot.

Arkell's aunt lived in the house from the age of two, and bought the property in 1979. On her death in the 1990s, the house passed to Julie, who now both lives and works in an interior steeped with personal history. With a degree in textiles and another in fashion textiles, there is something quite fitting about this artist living in a house built on Clothworkers' Company land. (A tailor is recorded, in 1907, as living a few doors down.) Arkell works in papier-mâché and mixed media, and has exhibited both at home and abroad. Her work often incorporates textiles in the form of old clothing, leftover balls of wool and scraps of ribbon, as well as items she discovered on inheriting the house.

Entering the house is like stepping into a children's classic, in a world of shoes and coats in the hall, cluttered nooks and crannies to be explored, and excitement on every floor as objects become curiouser and curiouser still. Only this is not a children's book, but a living and breathing house in 21st-century London. Positioned neatly on the uncarpeted stairs are soft-leather T-bar shoes, books and old toys, while a brightly spotted papier-mâché bug dangles mischievously from a scarcely visible string. The stairs continue up a floor to a busy landing, beyond which lies Arkell's studio. A battered chest of drawers carries

opposite Yellow walls and colourful pictures brighten up the steep and narrow staircase. Neatly placed, yet rather odd items such as a pair of baby shoes and a little bird's nest appear on the stairs at the next level.

below Occupied by a chest of drawers and a dressmaker's dummy, with countless items on the walls, the landing at the top of the stairs is an unexpectedly busy area.

JULIE ARKELL'S HOUSE

209

JULIE ARKELL'S HOUSE

opposite Purpose-built by the artist's partner, the studio shelving contains a multitude of found objects, toys and artists' materials.

above Many of the items in the studio are connected with Arkell's papier-mâché work, from huge rolls of brown paper to old newspapers.

soft toys, framed artworks, a lamp with knitted shade and fabric flowers in a vase. Plastic rabbit lights are draped around the doorway. Covered in pasted newspaper and dressed in knitted collar, paper beads and hoops, a dressmaker's dummy partly blocks the doorway, as if protecting the studio from unwanted visitors.

A large, well-lit top room, the studio is quite something. Minimalists would shudder; maximalists would glory in the sensory overload – especially those still in tune with their inner child. Everything begs further inspection, whether the artworks themselves or the very many assorted items that are also housed here. Baskets of wool, cotton reels, children's dresses, cloth bags, ribbons, woollen dolls' clothes and plastic dolls in little bags surround shelving containing art books, craft books and children's books. On the opposite wall is the floor-to-ceiling shelving that is visible from the landing, with jars of buttons, little pots of paint, knitted toys and rather scary plastic dolls' parts. Do not assume that quantity means chaos – this is an ordered space, with objects compartmentalised and categorised.

In the centre of the studio is the worktable, with paintbrushes, pencil pots and tubes of gouache. Arkell's work is entirely by hand, and ranges from making and

painting papier-mâché figures, animals and objects, to embroidering and knitting accessories and pasting on found objects.

Descending the stairs, the hall comes properly into view. Wicker bags and vintage dresses hang from walls and doors. A bookcase features such classics as *Swallows and Amazons*. Fabric roses adorn the hall lampshade. It is suddenly apparent that there are very few synthetic or modern materials here, save for the telephone/answering machine that one feels was installed with a certain sense of regret. This is a world with no email and no television. (There is no car either, but this is less unusual for a central London location.)

In the early 1970s, a major concession to modern living occurred in this house – a bathroom was installed. Before that, bathing involved a tin bath in the kitchen, a Formica counter being placed over the top when it was not in use. As there was nowhere obvious to locate the new bathroom, a central room in the house had to be converted. Its location is certainly a surprise, but the resulting room is rather appealing. Indications of its original use as a living space include the large sash window and beautiful iron fireplace. Tucked beside the chimney breast is the lavatory, while on the opposite wall are the bath, sink and cabinet. Playful and quirky, this is no ordinary bathroom wall.

The decor on the hall side of the same wall is quite different. Here, two wallpapers of old are in evidence, battered and faded. White flowers, old prints and children's imagery from the last century somehow combine to create the sense that this is a memorial to a lost child, or lost youth. After the light and playfulness of the bathroom, it is an unexpectedly dark space.

The basement floor is now a cheerful sitting-room area on the street side of the house, and an even more cheerful kitchen on the garden side. When Arkell

above left It is impossible not to smile when you see Arkell's papier-mâché characters gathered together on the table. They may still be in the process of being made, but already they look as if they have just got off the bus.

above right Entitled *Two Poets Searching for Words*, this work of papier-mâché, wool and a recycled tourist map is finished off by a stick with the word 'contents' attached. To the right is a work entitled *Bunnies in a Drawer*.

opposite, top left Amongst the scraps of material and cuttings is a set of three animals entitled *Rabbit Donkeys*.

opposite, top right The stretch of hall wall along the stairs to the basement is a strange section of the house, with assorted images of childhood hung against old wallpapers.

opposite, below Old bottles, shells, angels, mermaids and candleholders on the whitewashed walls of the bathroom create a timeless tableau.

JULIE ARKELL'S HOUSE

JULIE ARKELL'S HOUSE

above left Old-fashioned tins, retro canisters for tea, coffee and sugar, and a classic blue-and-white striped milk jug adorn the shelves of the simple, wooden kitchen dresser.

above right A small wooden shelf with narrow bottom drawer has been brightly decorated with predominantly red and yellow objects, topped by cutouts of Van Dyck children.

opposite In the living room, carved wooden toys and a colourful circular carpet sit in front of the decorative iron fireplace. High above the cards, books and flowers on the mantelpiece is a stunning light shade of colourful rosettes and paper tickets.

below Postcards on the windowsill ensure that even the kitchen sink is not a particularly conventional space in the house.

inherited the house, this area had to be gutted due to damp. Layers of magnolia woodchip were stripped out, and a Somerset-stone floor laid.

The focus of the living room is the chimney breast, with wooden fire surround and patchwork sections pinned to a length of picture rail. Appropriately, a leaflet about Dennis Severs' House (see separate section) is currently propped on the mantelpiece. A comfortable sofa faces the fireplace, and all around are books, toys and artworks.

The kitchen window is small, and garden foliage grows thickly close by, but apple-green walls lift this potentially gloomy area to create one of crisp freshness. Brightly coloured objects are displayed on shelving units of reclaimed wood, and the by now familiar collection of toys and pictures hangs on the wall. This is a friendly space, and the greenery at the window adds to the cottage-like appeal.

For a recent exhibition at London's Contemporary Applied Arts gallery, Arkell wrote: 'I respond to the imperfection of things. Something frayed, faded, stained or coming undone has more meaning for me than an object perfectly put together.' This approach to her art must relate directly to her lifelong association with a house that was never 'done up'. With titles like *The Cloud Collector*, *Rabbit Poet* and *In Pursuit of Jam*, her works are imbued with a sense of dreamy wistfulness, and there is something of this in the house, too. House and art are irrevocably bound together, making this an interior of endless charm and fascination.

STYLE GUIDE

Since the essence of eccentric style is that of an unorthodox approach to design, these pages are more about inspiring individual creativity than setting a specific style template. The four themes below provide key visual categories that emerge from the wide range of projects cited in this book, and serve as a brief selection of sources for enjoyable and fulfilling interior design.

Unless specified otherwise, the organisations listed are based in the UK. However, all have websites, and most are aimed at an international audience.

COUNTRY HOUSE

RESOURCES AND COLLECTIONS

Historic Houses Association
www.hha.org.uk
Represents historic houses, castles and gardens in the UK that remain in private ownership. (The majority provide some form of public access.) Includes Southside House and Capesthorne Hall.

Country Life
www.countrylife.co.uk
Magazine and website, including articles on historic houses, interior design and properties for sale.

The National Trust
www.nationaltrust.org.uk
Charity that protects and opens to the public British historic houses, gardens, industrial monuments and mills.

The Stately Homes Guide
www.stately-homes.com
Website designed to help with planning visits to, or events at, Britain's stately homes, gardens, castles and other historic properties.

DESIGNERS AND SUPPLIERS

Colefax & Fowler
www.colefax.com
English fabrics and wallpapers, used in many country houses as well as contemporary 'twists' such as 43 South Molton Street. Website includes worldwide list of stockists.

Ian Walton Associates
www.iddv.com/ianwalton
Interior design company best known for its 'Comfortable English Country House Style'.

Strawberry Fool
www.strawberryfool.co.uk
Unusual and attractive items for sale, such as enamel rustic kitchenware.

Made in Sheffield Dot Com
www.madeinsheffield.com
Fine Sheffield silverware and pewterware, from cutlery to candlesticks.

Simply Footstools
www.simplyfootstools.co.uk
Footstools handcrafted in Scotland.

THEATRICAL

RESOURCES AND COLLECTIONS

Sir John Soane's Museum
www.soane.org
Soane designed this house to live in, but
also as a dramatic setting for his
antiquities and works of art.

Paul Corin's Magnificent Music Machines
www.chycor.co.uk/tourism/paul-corin-
music
A delightfully eccentric museum created
on the back of one man's passion for
music boxes, Wurlitzers and organs of
yesteryear.

The Theatre Museum
www.theatremuseum.org.uk
Wide range of documents, artefacts and
works of art that record the history of the
performing arts in Britain from the 16th
century to the present day.

The Billy Rose Theatre Collection, US
www.nypl.org/research/lpa/the/the.html
Archive at the New York Public Library
devoted to the theatrical arts. An
extensive resource for artists, writers and
researchers as well as the general public.

Art Crimes, US
www.graffiti.org
Online gallery of graffiti art from cities
around the world.

DESIGNERS AND SUPPLIERS

DistinctlyBritish.com
www.distinctlybritish.com
Website bringing together creative small
producers of high-quality British goods,
from Gothic bird tables to themed dinner-
party packs such as a Shakespeare
banquet.

Osborne & Little
www.osborneandlittle.com
Asian- and antique-inspired fabrics and
wallpapers. Website includes worldwide
list of stockists.

Revamp Interiors
www.revampinteriors.co.uk
Interiors for mansions, luxury yachts,
houses, hotels and restaurants. Suppliers
of curtains and upholstery for Rules
Restaurant & Private Rooms, where
antique gold trim on burgundy wool
velvet maintains the theatrical look.

Totally Funky
www.totally-funky.co.uk
Humorous items for the home.

Salvo
www.salvoweb.com
British directory of dealers in architectural
salvage, garden antiques and reclaimed
building materials.

MAXIMALIST

RESOURCES AND COLLECTIONS

Linley Sambourne House
www.rbkc.gov.uk/linleysambournehouse
Late Victorian townhouse, furnished in the
'aesthetic', or artistic, style. The house
survives with almost all of its furniture
and fittings intact.

Snowshill Manor
www.nationaltrust.org.uk/places/snowshill
manor
The eccentric home of thousands of art
and design treasures, collected between
1900 and 1951 by architect and craftsman
Charles Paget Wade.

Pitt Rivers Museum
www.prm.ox.ac.uk
Cluttered cases and original handwritten
labels display textiles, masks, musical
instruments, jewellery, weapons and tools
grouped according to type rather than
period to give an excellent social history.

**Period Living and Traditional Homes
Magazine**
www.periodliving.co.uk
Inspiration and advice from decoration to
renovation, plus an invaluable directory of
suppliers.

Maxalot, Spain
www.maxalot.com
International community of individuals on
the cutting edge of maximalist art, from
graphic design to street art. The collective
showcases works at its main gallery in
Barcelona.

DESIGNERS AND SUPPLIERS

The Antique Lighting Company
www.antiquelights.co.uk
Genuine English antique lights and lamps,
mostly Victorian and Edwardian, including
Art Nouveau and Arts and Crafts designs.

La Maison
www.atlamaison.com
Antique and reproduction French
bedroom furniture, as seen at the Great
John Street Hotel.

The Dream Scene
www.thedreamscene.com
Unique wallpaper murals, including
trompe l'oeil colonnaded vistas and wildly
colourful children's designs.

Fabric World
www.fabricworldlondon.co.uk
Described by the store as an Aladdin's
cave of designer fabrics.

Timorous Beasties
www.timorousbeasties.co.uk
Shop and design studio, run by a Scottish
duo who have been described as 'textile
mavericks'. Traditional textiles and
wallpapers feature designs that cross
many disciplines and styles.

Sara Bengur Associates, US
www.sarabengur.com
Maximalist interior designer, known for
extravagant combinations of textiles old
and new.

HERITAGE

RESOURCES AND COLLECTIONS

Geffrye Museum
www.geffrye-museum.org.uk
Period rooms showing the changing style
of the English domestic interior from 1600
to the present day.

Victoria and Albert Museum
www.vam.ac.uk
The British Galleries display a
comprehensive collection of British art
and design from 1500 to 1900.

York Castle Museum
www.yorkcastlemuseum.org.uk
The Museum houses a remarkable
collection of British household items
from 1600 to 2002.

The Landmark Trust
www.landmarktrust.org.uk
Charity that rescues and restores historic
buildings and converts them into holiday
accommodation. Properties include the
Bath House, Gothic Temple and
Beckford's Tower.

English Heritage
www.english-heritage.org.uk
The UK government's statutory adviser on
the historic environment, which lists
buildings for protection. Courthouse Hotel
Kempinski is an example.

**Cooper-Hewitt National Design
Museum, US**
www.ndm.si.edu
Includes 18th- and early 19th-century
English printed fabrics, and the largest
collection of wall coverings in the US.

DESIGNERS AND SUPPLIERS

Limelight
www.limelightgb.com
Wrought-ironwork, antique wall lighting,
chandeliers, strap hinges, latches, curtain
poles and rosehead nails. Order online or
visit the old timber-framed showroom.

Liberty
www.liberty.co.uk
The famous store has recently opened
a new furniture section – 'Design
1850–1950' – selling Arts and Crafts
items as objects for contemporary
use in the home.

Sanderson
www.sanderson-uk.com
Fabrics and wallpapers plus the William
Morris Archive. Website includes
worldwide list of stockists.

Stuart Interiors
www.stuartinteriors.ltd.uk
Tudor-, medieval- and Georgian-style
interior designers, plus expert historical
research and restoration.

Robert Kime
www.robertkime.com
Designer, restorer and dealer for private
clients. Sells fabrics and furniture, old and
new, to those who visit his farm buildings
on a remote hill in Wiltshire.

George Smith, US
www.georgesmith.com
Vintage-style and eccentric fabrics
and furniture.

James Ayres, *Domestic Interiors: The British Tradition 1500–1850,* Yale University Press (London), 2003.

Quentin Bell and Virginia Nicholson, *Charleston: A Bloomsbury House and Garden*, Frances Lincoln Ltd (London), 2004.

E Borish, Louise Cooper, Steve Morgan, Peter J Murray, Cristina Palomares: *Strangest Pubs in Britain*, Strangest Books (Birmingham), 2002.

Stephen Calloway and Elizabeth Collins Cromley (eds), *The Elements of Style: An Encyclopedia of Domestic Architectural Detail*, Mitchell Beazley (London), 2005.

Ian Chilvers and Harold Osborne (eds), *The Oxford Dictionary of Art*, Oxford University Press (Oxford), 2004.

John Cornforth, *London Interiors: From the Archives of Country Life*, Aurum Press (London), 2000.

James Stevens Curl, *Georgian Architecture*, David & Charles (Newton Abbot), 1996.

Jean-Claude Delormé, *Architects' Dream Houses*, Abbeville Press (New York), 1996.

Mark Fisher, *Britain's Best Museums and Galleries*, Allen Lane (London), 2004.

Philippa Glanville and Hilary Young, *Elegant Eating: 400 Years of Dining in Style*, V&A Publications (London), 2004.

Des Hannigan, *Eccentric Britain*, New Holland (London), 2004.

Anna Jackson, *The V&A Guide to Period Styles*, V&A Publications (London), 2005.

Simon Jenkins, *England's Thousand Best Houses*, Allen Lane (London), 2003.

Fiona Leslie, *Designs for 20th-Century Interiors*, V&A Publications (London), 2003.

Philippa Lewis, *Details: A Guide to House Design in Britain*, Prestel Publishing (London), 2003.

Jeremy Musson, *How to Read a Country House*, Ebury Press (London), 2005.

Dennis Severs, *18 Folgate Street: The Tale of a House in Spitalfields*, Vintage (London), 2002.

Michael Snodin and John Styles, *Design and the Decorative Arts: Britain 1500–1900*, V&A Publications (London), 2001.

James Stourton, *Great Smaller Museums of Europe*, Scala Publishers (London), 2003.

Gordon Thorburn, *Men and Sheds*, New Holland (London), 2003.

Peter Thornton, *Authentic Decor: The Domestic Interior, 1620–1920*, Weidenfeld & Nicolson (London), 2000.

Simon Thurley, *Lost Buildings of Britain*, Viking (London), 2004.

Howard Watson, *Hotel Revolution: 21st-Century Hotel Design*, John Wiley and Sons Ltd (Chichester), 2005.

Michael Webb, *Art/Invention/House*, Rizzoli International Publications (New York), 2005.

FURTHER READING